DISTILLED IN
OREGON

A HISTORY & GUIDE
with Cocktail Recipes

SCOTT STURSA

Foreword by Margarett Waterbury of **Edible Portland**

AMERICAN PALATE

Published by American Palate
A Division of The History Press
Charleston, SC
www.historypress.net

Back cover, background: Courtesy of Hood River Distillers.

First published 2017

Manufactured in the United States

ISBN 9781467137720

Library of Congress Control Number: 2016953501

To Kathy
I still don't know why she puts up with me.

CONTENTS

FOREWORD

Well Portland, Oregon, and sloe gin fizz
If that ain't love then tell me what is
Well I lost my heart it didn't take no time
But that ain't all. I lost my mind in Oregon.
—*Loretta Lynn*

Distilling attracts a certain kind of person. I won't use the word *crazy*, but let's just say crazy isn't a disqualifier.

Good distillers are willing to spend long hours doing hard, expensive, messy work on the off-chance that the result, years later, will be something that brings a bit of pleasure to other people. It's not a profession for everybody, but for some, it's more than a job—it's a calling.

Right now, Oregon is home to a lot of those people. Over the past fifteen years, the craft distilling industry has grown so dramatically that you'd be forgiven for thinking it sprang forth, fully formed, from the turn of the twenty-first century like Athena did from Zeus's head.

In reality, Oregon distillers have been engaged in that most mundane of alchemies, turning grain and fruit into alcohol, for hundreds of years. In the early days of Oregon history, local distilleries were commonplace, and small-scale agricultural distilling—using stills to preserve surplus crops, for pleasure and profit—was just common sense. Before railroads, the best—sometimes the only—way to get whiskey was to make it yourself.

FOREWORD

The giant eraser of Prohibition not only wiped most of those small distilleries off the map, it wiped our collective consciousness clean of the memory of regional distilling. That's our loss. The diversity of regional distilling, once alive and well, enlivened our communities with local flavors, local color and, yes—oh, yes—some seriously entertaining local personalities. Horse thieves, corrupt sheriffs, lowlife saloonkeepers, tax dodgers—they're all here.

Fortunately, some of that diversity is coming back. Our current distillery landscape might confound a time traveler from 1955, but one from 1855 would feel right at home.

Scott Stursa puts the Oregon distillery boom into valuable perspective with this rigorously researched glimpse into our state's boozy past, from the unscrupulous Hudson's Bay Company employee who flavored rum with a bit of grain and called it "whiskey"—its nickname, "Blue Ruin," does seem more appropriate—all the way through today's quality-obsessed entrepreneurs, making brandy one pear at a time. It's a spirited history that's simultaneously scholarly and lively, grounded and opinionated, all leavened with a touch of dry humor and an obvious delight in the quirky details of the historical record.

It's a good time to be a drinker in Oregon. Is it a good time to be a distiller? Perhaps. Honestly, it has never been easy. Take the Portland Distilling and Cattle Feeding Company. Built in 1891, it was totally destroyed not once but twice in the next three years: burned to the ground in 1892 and then swept away in the 1894 flood—twelve employees and all. It's enough to make today's tribulations with federal labeling legislation and facilities regulations seem minor by comparison. Instead of glossing over the challenges, Stursa confronts them head on, offering a no-BS glimpse into the trials of taking up the mash paddle.

Running a still connects you to a fraternity that spans eons. When today's distillers make a heads cut, tighten a barrel hoop or adjust the pH of their mash to accommodate a surprisingly acidic wild yeast on the skins of the plums they harvested from a friend's farm, they're walking in a well-worn set of footsteps—footsteps that trace the many paths Oregonians walked before they got here: from Germany, from Boston, from Georgia, from England and from farther afield.

Between then and now, the colorful characters, the entrepreneurs, the bon vivants, the misfits and, yes, the swindlers are the same. Times may have changed, but there has always been something about Oregon that attracts distillers. It's one of the only states able to grow grain and

FOREWORD

fruit with equal faculty, and abundant pure water sources from Cascade Mountain snowpack, a flowing network of rivers and our famous rains have kept mash tuns and worm tubs full for generations

Plus, I think there's something special in Oregon that's long been a kind of psychic Bat-Signal for the fanatical, the hyper-focused, the dream-chaser, the geek, the oddball—the kind of person who makes a good distiller, craziness and all. *Distilled in Oregon* brings all those characters together in one place for the very first time, and you're invited to the party.

MARGARETT WATERBURY
Editor
Edible Portland Magazine

ACKNOWLEDGEMENTS

Thank you to the staff at the Oregon State Archives, the Oregon Historical Society, the Southern Oregon Historical Society, the Columbia Gorge Discovery Center, the Polk County Historical Society and the National Archives in Seattle.

Thank you to Steve McCarthy and all the other Oregon distillers who shared their stories with me.

Thank you to Elizabeth Dameron, great-granddaughter of one of the founders of Hood River Distillers, for the information she provided and for permission to use her photographs.

Thank you to Christie Scott and Joy Spencer of the Oregon Liquor Control Commission.

Thank you to all the friends who supported me and, in particular, to Lyn Larson for her help in editing the draft manuscript.

And thank you most of all to my wife, Kathleen, for believing in me and for excusing me from numerous household duties so that I could finish this by deadline.

THIS BOOK IS OBSOLETE!

O K, just the final chapter, which attempts to provide a brief description of all the distilleries that have opened in Oregon since 2009, is outdated. Between the time that this book was submitted to the publisher and the time it appeared in print, there will have been at least four more distillery openings, possibly more—not to mention all the distilleries that will open in the years following publication. I'll try to keep track of them and post updates to www.distilledinoregon.com.

When I first conceived of this book (in late 2011), my initial thought was to publish a guide to the currently operating distilleries in the state, rather like a winery guide. However, with only about twenty distilleries operating at the time, it would have made for a slim book. I decided instead to do a full historical treatment, reaching back to the 1830s. The result was a lot of time spent at historical archives, and by the time I finished (in August 2016), there were over sixty distilleries in Oregon, more than enough for a guide.

But I have no regrets about the historical research and content. It's a great story, starting with the fur traders who were distilling "blue ruin" in the 1830s and moving to the whiskey distillers of the 1880s and 1890s, the progress and ultimate success of the state's prohibition movement, the founding of Hood River Distillers after Prohibition and the story of Steve McCarthy and Clear Creek Distillery. It is full of many fascinating stories and colorful characters.

INTRODUCTION

This is not to say that the modern era does not include fascinating stories and colorful characters, and I'm including as many as I can in chapters 10 through 12. In chapter 12, I'll also address the question of why Oregon seems to be at the forefront of the craft distilling movement—because it is, you know, and someone needed to get the story out there. I'm glad I was able to do it.

SCOTT STURSA
August 22, 2016

1

DISTILLED SPIRITS

A QUICK PRIMER

Before commencing my account of distilling in Oregon, I'm providing a brief overview of distillation and of the various types of spirits produced by distillers, the intent being to avoid disrupting the narrative with descriptive digressions. For example, in chapter 2, when I note that Conner was producing not whiskey but wheat-flavored rum, I don't want to detour into an explanation of how those differ, so I'm doing that here.

Spirits distillation relies on the different boiling points of ethyl alcohol (ethanol) and water, the former being 173 degrees Fahrenheit and the latter being 212 degrees Fahrenheit. Heat any alcohol-containing beverage (beer or wine) to a temperature between these two, and only the ethanol will boil off. The actual process of distilling spirits is a little more complicated; generally, a distillation run consists of gradually heating the fermented material and monitoring the output from the still. As the contents of the still approach 173 degrees, a variety of volatile compounds begin to emerge. These include acetone and methanol, neither of which you want in your cocktail (unless you're a native of Saturn's moon Titan, in which case I expect you'll also want a dash of ammonia and a spritz of methane with it). This head portion of the run is diverted and used for other purposes (such as removing stubborn stains). Toward the end of the run, as the temperature approaches 212 degrees, the output becomes increasingly watery, and this tail is likewise diverted.

DISTILLED IN OREGON

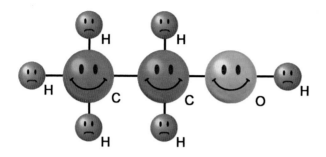

Ethyl alcohol. The hydrogen atoms lack smiles because hydrogen is a sullen, bitter element, believing itself unfairly blamed for the Hindenburg disaster.

You'd expect the part between the head and tail to be called the body, but you'd be wrong. It's instead called the heart, and many double-distilled spirits are described as being "from the heart of the heart" (admittedly "from the body of the body" just sounds creepy).

The original type of still used for distilling is known as a pot still, a simple device consisting of a closed container (the pot) that contains the fermented material. As this is heated, the alcohol vaporizes and rises to the top, where it is diverted into a coil of tubular copper or stainless steel (the worm). Here it cools and condenses, and the output is collected as it exits the coil.

This type of still cannot produce spirits much stronger than 80 percent ABV (alcohol by volume), although multiple distillation (returning the spirit to the still and repeating the process) can raise this to 85 to 90 percent. This is sufficient for most traditional spirits because if you want the character of the original raw material (grapes, apples, barley, whatever) to show up in the final product, then you don't want to distill it any stronger than 70 percent ABV.

A pot still is a type of batch still, so called because the product is produced in batches. After a run, the contents of the pot must be removed, the still cleaned and a new batch of fermented material added before the next run begins.

In the early 1800s, a new type of still was devised, the column still. The workings of these are rather complex, and I'm not going to describe them here. The important things to remember about the column still are 1) it can run continuously, and 2) it can produce spirits as strong as 95 to 96 percent ABV. Spirits produced at 95 percent ABV or higher are known as neutral spirits, so called because, at this level, supposedly no character of the original raw material remains. I say "supposedly" because those with a keen sense of smell can often pick up a little aroma, and if the spirit was made from a particularly pungent material, such as molasses, then most people can smell it.

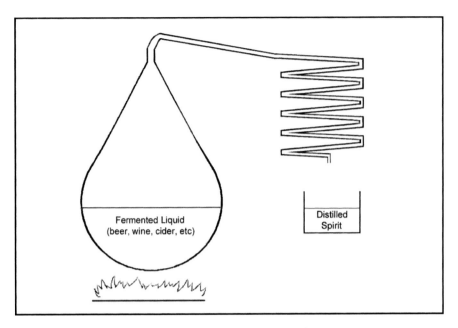

Fermented Liquid
(beer, wine, cider, etc)

Distilled
Spirit

A pot still, so simple a hillbilly can build one. *Diagram by the author.*

There are all sorts of variations in the design of both pot and column stills, and there is even a hybrid type, essentially a pot still with a column on top (these are known as reflux stills). This type is favored by many craft distillers, who often call them pot stills. Although they operate in batch mode, they are not, strictly speaking, pot stills.

Distillation was discovered in the first century AD by alchemists in Alexandria, the scientific center of the Roman Empire (another resident of the city designed and built an early type of steam engine). Like steam power, distillation was viewed mostly as a curiosity, and the Romans didn't do much with it (just as well, as the combination of Caligula and gin would have considerably hastened the demise of the empire).

After the collapse of civilization in western Europe, much of the Romans' knowledge was preserved by Islamic scholars and alchemists, who distilled spirits for medicines and perfumes, and if they sampled it at all, did so only to ensure its purity (of course).

The science of distillation began to spread to Christian Europe in the late middle ages. In the French districts of Armagnac and Cognac, where the mediocre quality of the wine made it uncompetitive with wine from neighboring Bordeaux, the locals discovered distilling their bad wine created a product that found a receptive market. To this day, the French like to say "the worst grapes make the best brandy" (they also claim to build reliable automobiles). Farther north, in the Calvados district of Normandy, the producers of hard apple cider made a similar discovery.

The French called these fruit-based spirits eau de vie ("water of life"), and while it's true they were clear and colorless, they certainly did not go down like water. However, like most liquid products of the era, they were put in barrels for storage or transport, and it was quickly appreciated that time in wood gave the spirit a mellower character, as well as imparting a warm golden color.

One of the export markets for the French spirits was the Netherlands, where it was known as *brandewijn* ("burned wine"), a word that eventually evolved into *brandy*. Thus, while eau de vie and brandy are technically synonymous, in modern usage the former is used to designate unaged (colorless) fruit spirits, and the latter is used for those having spent time in a barrel.

Grappa (in France known as *marc*) is a type of eau de vie made from pomace, the skins, pulp, seeds and stems left over from winemaking. Traditionally made to provide the peasantry with affordable brandy, in the 1990s a number of Italian producers discovered the combination of ignorance, the word "imported" and the use of a fancy bottle would achieve significant sales in the United States. This is not to say there isn't some decent grappa being made, both in Italy and in the United States, but most European grappa is swill.

Distilling eventually reached Ireland and Scotland, where there wasn't much wine but plenty of beer, so beer is what was poured into the still. The Irish and Scots also called their spirit "water of life," which in Gaelic is *uisce beatha*. The first of these two words is pronounced "iss-kee" and eventually evolved into the word *whiskey*.

Like the French brandy makers, the whiskey producers also discovered time in the barrel improved their product.

Because yeast cannot work on a plain grain mash, at least a portion of it must be malted. Malting refers to the process of allowing the grain to germinate prior to drying, grinding and mashing. The germination process creates enzymes in the grain that convert starch to sugar, allowing yeast to convert the sugar to alcohol. Because the action of these enzymes is catalytic, they are not used up in the process and will eventually convert all the starch in a mash, even that which is unmalted.

Malted barley contains more of these enzymes than most grains and is particularly efficient at starch-to-sugar conversion. For this reason, it's used in the production of nearly every whiskey, be it Irish (partly grain barley), bourbon (mostly corn), rye whiskey (mostly rye) or Canadian (usually mostly rye but not always). The only large distillery not using malt is Alberta Springs (Calgary, Canada), which uses an enzyme extracted from *Aspergillus* fungus. Many craft distillers use this as well.

Some whiskeys are made entirely from malted grain; these are known as malt whiskeys. The term *single malt* means the whiskey came from a single distillery, as opposed to a blend of malt whiskeys from multiple distilleries.

Rice being a grain, a fermented beverage made from it is technically a beer. But because the method used to make sake, using *Aspergillus* fungus and specific types of yeast, produces alcohol levels much higher than most beer, sake is commonly called rice wine (that, plus it lacks bubbles). Again, because rice is a grain, a distilled spirit made from it is technically a whiskey. In China, locally distilled grain spirits are known as *baijiu* (pronounced "Bye Joe"), and those made from rice are considered a subtype of baijiu (others are made from barley or millet, and most baijiu is made from sorghum). The Korean equivalent of baijiu is *soju*, and in Japan, it's known as *shochu*, and the rice-based version is called *kome*.

In the 1500s, the Dutch developed a spirit known as *Genever* (Dutch for juniper). A freshly distilled batch of grain spirit (usually malted rye and barley) would be redistilled in a still containing a tray of crushed juniper berries along with a number of herbs and spices (known as the "botanicals"). The alcohol vapor would pass through the tray, picking up the flavor of the berries and botanicals. This spirit was an immediate hit, particularly among English troops sent to the Netherlands by Elizabeth I to assist the Dutch in their war of independence. The English called it "gen" for short, and this word evolved into *gin* (it was also called "Dutch courage," which either meant you needed courage to drink it or meant drinking it enhanced your courage, or possibly both).

Gin production was undertaken with enthusiasm in England. Cheap to make, it was immensely popular with people of limited means, and the resulting "gin craze" of the early 1700s led to numerous acts of Parliament intended to control its consumption. Without exception, these failed.

When the column still was introduced in the 1800s, English gin producers began using the higher-alcohol spirit produced by these. The result was a lighter, drier style of gin, becoming known as London dry gin.

In eastern Europe and Russia, there was little appreciation for flavored and/or aged spirits, with the main goal being to minimize the time between pouring the spirit and getting it into one's stomach. Aroma and taste were therefore irrelevant. *Vodka* (a Russian term meaning "little water") was initially made in pot stills, using multiple passes through the still (at least three). But with the introduction of the column still, production was simplified, and everyone—even the peasants—could afford it. Modern vodka is a neutral spirit watered down to 40 to 50 percent ABV. Most vodkas use neutral spirits made from grain, but it can actually be made from anything (potatoes, molasses, sugar beets, whatever).

The New World has added a couple of selections to the spirits lineup, one based on an indigenous source and the other on an introduced one. The first of these sources is agave, the sap of which was being fermented by the Aztecs into a beverage known as pulque. Pulque is an acquired taste, one the Spanish were unable to acquire, so they tried running it through a still. The result was no better than pulque itself. Noting that a favorite dish of the natives, the roasted heart of the agave, was rather sweet, they chopped, pulped, fermented and distilled some of these. The output was still a rather rough spirit but was better than distilled pulque, and became known as mezcal (or, if it conforms to certain compositional and geographic standards, tequila).

Not long after Europeans colonized the West Indies, sugar cane was introduced, and by the early 1600s, most of the islands had a large number of sugar plantations. Molasses is a byproduct of sugar production, and there being only a limited market for it, most of it was fed to livestock or simply dumped. Eventually, an enterprising plantation owner hit on the idea of adding warm water and yeast to it and, after fermentation completed, running it through a still. The resulting spirit was called rumbullion, and later shortened to rum (also called killdevil, probably because some of this early rum was so bad it was believed that enough of it would kill anything).

Some rum is made from fresh-pressed cane juice, some is made from white or brown sugar and some is made from cane syrup. But most is made from molasses. Rum is probably made in a wider variety of styles than any other spirit, ranging from light white rums to heavy dark ones to brandy-like ones made from cane juice and aged for more than twelve years in French oak (some people like to call these last "Caribbean cognac" and, in fact, they often taste more like brandy than rum).

The final major category of spirit is liqueur (also known as cordials). These are made by taking a base spirit (usually, but not always, brandy or neutral spirit), adding a sweetener (sugar, honey, some type of syrup) and optional flavoring. Liqueurs can be simple (most whiskey-based liqueurs involve nothing more than adding honey to the whiskey) to bewilderingly complex (Chartreuse, created by Carthusian monks in the early 1700s as a medicinal elixir, contains over one hundred ingredients). In the United States (and only the United States), liqueurs using a brandy base can be labeled "flavored brandy." This unfortunate practice has led many to believe that brandy itself is sweet.

Schnapps, in Germany, is a generic term that can be applied to any distilled spirit. In the United States, schnapps is usually a liqueur using a neutral spirits base. These have usually, but not always, a higher proof than most liqueurs.

The plethora of flavored vodkas currently crowding liquor store shelves are not liqueurs because they are not sweetened.

These descriptions are as brief as I can make them and still be reasonably accurate. Purists will undoubtedly decry them as oversimplified, but this is as much space as I want to devote to this. I (and hopefully you as well) would like to get on with our story.

So, a quick review:

> **brandy**: made from grapes or other fruit; in unaged form is known as **eau de vie**.

> **whiskey**: made from grain, a portion of which is usually malted.

> **gin**: neutral spirit infused with juniper and botanicals.

> **vodka**: neutral spirit diluted with water.

> **mezcal/tequila**: made from agave.

> **rum**: made from sugar cane.

> **liqueur**: any of the above with sweetener and optional flavoring added.

So now that you're suitably informed, we can get on with our story.

2

BLUE RUIN

Lewis and Clark wintered at the mouth of the Columbia in 1805–6, building a camp called Fort Clatsop (the Clatsop being the local tribe of Chinook-speaking natives). During the next few years, the only whites visiting the area were wandering fur-trappers, and it wasn't until 1811 that they established their first permanent presence, that being Fort Astoria (located, as you might have guessed, on the same site as the present-day town of Astoria). Constructed and operated by John Jacob Astor's Pacific Fur Company, the enterprise was not particularly successful, and in 1813, local management sold it to the British-owned North West Company. This was during the War of 1812, and shortly thereafter, the British warship *Raccoon* arrived with orders to capture the fort. Finding it already in British hands, Captain William Black nonetheless made a great show of raising an American flag, lowering it and raising a British one (any Clatsop observing this had to be questioning the sanity of white people).[1]

In 1821, the North West Company was acquired by another British firm, the Hudson's Bay Company (HBC), and when the regional manager of HBC visited in 1824, he expressed dissatisfaction with the location of the fort and ordered that a new one be built farther upriver. Construction of Fort Vancouver began that same year, and Dr. John McLoughlin was put in charge (a position he kept for another twenty-two years).

HBC wanted the colony to be self-sufficient, so McLoughlin immediately began planting wheat, vegetables and apple and peach trees. It was discovered that the European wine grape, *Vitis vinifera*, flourished here, unlike in the eastern part of the continent, where it quickly succumbed to phylloxera and various fungal blights. An experimental crop of barley planted in 1826 yielded a harvest exceeding expectations, and brewing began later that same year. By 1829, one of McLoughlin's lieutenants, while in Hawaii, announced that Vancouver would soon be exporting beer (trade with Hawaii commenced early on, with surplus agricultural production being exported to the islands and sugar, molasses and guest workers being imported).[2]

In 1829, the scale of operations (tanning, milling, lumber production and more) exceeded the capacity of the fort, and the town of Vancouver was founded outside its walls. Within a few years, its inhabitants exceeded six hundred in number, with a polyglot population composed of Englishmen, Scots, French Canadians, Hawaiians and native peoples (including Iroquois from back East).

With so many people arriving in the area, it was inevitable that some would arrive infected with disease, and during the winter of 1828–29, smallpox and measles swept through the native Chinook population. The mortality rate approached 90 percent.

The resulting availability of unpopulated territory encouraged an expansion of settlement, and in 1829, Etienne Lucier, an ex-employee of Hudson's Bay Company, started a farm on the east bank of the Willamette River, at a location that today is in downtown Portland. Over the next few years, settlement gradually worked its way up the Willamette Valley, with the new inhabitants including a good number of Americans, the region being under a "mutual occupancy" agreement between the United States and Great Britain (a not totally harmonious arrangement; think "joint custody").

In 1833, a distillery was constructed in Vancouver. Old maps show it being on the Columbia waterfront, near the current location of Joe's Crab Shack.[3] What was being produced there is unknown, but there was certainly no shortage of raw material—apple cider and wine for brandy, beer for whiskey and Hawaiian molasses for rum—and it probably absorbed any surplus of all of these commodities.

The year 1834 saw the arrival of Methodist missionaries, led by Jason Lee of New York. They established several missions, the largest being near present-day Salem.

In 1836, the Vancouver distillery ceased operation. McLoughlin based the decision on "the bad effect it had on our affairs" and further stated that he "would recommend if possible never to attempt it again."[4] The "bad effects" were probably an undermining of HBC's relationship with the Chinook; in all likelihood, a portion of the distillery's output found its

Fort Vancouver, circa 1855. *Courtesy Library of Congress, LC-USZ62-31252.*

way to these people, and tribal leaders, observing the debilitating effect it had on their members, complained to HBC authorities. Good relations with the natives being essential to the fur trade, McLoughlin probably felt he had no other choice.

The fundamental law of economics is that when there is a demand, there will be a supply. There was certainly a demand for distilled spirits, so it was inevitable that someone would step forward to provide a new supply. That someone was Ewing Young, a successful trapper and trader who had arrived in 1834, settling on the west bank of the Willamette across from the now abandoned community of Champoeg. Young had a rather unsavory reputation; among his alleged misdeeds was the theft of two hundred horses in California, and John McLoughlin had issued orders to HBC personnel to have no dealings with him.

In late 1836, Young and partner Lawrence Carmichael began constructing a distillery on Sauvie Island, across the river and downstream from Vancouver. This triggered a reaction among a number of people (including Reverend Lee), both those concerned about the sale of spirits to the natives and those who were followers of the temperance movement, a number of whom immediately met to form the first chapter of the Oregon Temperance Society.

It should be mentioned that at this point in its history, the temperance movement was exactly that; its members advocated temperance, not total abstinence. The movement was inspired by the writings of Dr. Benjamin Rush, who described the effects of cider, beer and wine as "cheerfulness, strength and nourishment, when taken only at meals, and in moderate quantities," while the effects of distilled spirits included, among other things, "Death, Suicide and Hatred of Just Government."

John McLoughlin. *Public domain.*

Young and Carmichael produced their first batch of spirits in December. One of Jason Lee's missionaries, a Reverend Frost, claimed that the product had no intoxicating "kick," but I suspect this was a propaganda ploy intended to discourage its purchase.

On January 2, 1837, Reverend Lee, the Temperance Society and twenty-two nonmembers (including Etienne Lucier) offered to buy out the operation, pledging to cover all of Young and Carmichael's expenses to date. In his reply, dated January 13, Young wrote:

Gentlemen,

Having taken into consideration your request to relinquish our enterprise in manufacturing ardent spirits we therefore do agree to stop our proceedings for the present. But Gentlemen the reasons for our first beginning such an undertaking was the innumerable difficulties and tyrannizing oppression of the Hudson's Bay Company here under the absolute authority of Dr. McLoughlin, who has treated us with more disdain than any American Citizen's feelings could support. But as there have now some favorable circumstances occurred that we can get along without making spirituous liquors, we resolve to stop the manufacture of it for the present.

Gentlemen, we do not feel it consistent with our feelings to receive any recompense whatever for our expenditures, but are thankful to the Society for their offer.

We remain yours &c
Young & Carmichael[5]

What were these "favorable circumstances"? It seems Reverend Lee, a man savvy enough to know Young wouldn't abandon his distillery unless there was a more lucrative alternative, had visited Young and pitched a proposal: Young would go to California and return with a herd of cattle. Doing this would break HBC's cattle monopoly (the company had built up a large herd over the years but refused to sell live cattle to anyone), and Lee knew Young would welcome an opportunity to take business away from the British company. On his visit to Young, Lee was accompanied by William Slacum of the U.S. Navy, who offered to transport Young to California at no cost.

So Young, Lee and other investors joined forces to form the Willamette Cattle Company, with Young at its head. Slacum took Young and ten associates to California on the USS *Loriot*, and Young purchased 630 head of cattle and drove them north to Oregon, opening the Siskiyou Trail in the process. He subsequently used some of his profits to convert his distillery into a sawmill.

For the moment, production of distilled spirits in Oregon had ceased.

The next relevant event in our tale concerns one Dr. Elijah White, who had arrived by ship in 1836. Jason Lee hired him to act as the mission's resident physician, but over the next several years, it became apparent to Lee that White was an individual of questionable morality; he dismissed White in the late summer of 1840. White subsequently boarded the next ship for New York.

In February 1841, Ewing Young died, with no heir and no will. By this time, he was the wealthiest man in Oregon, with both debtors and creditors, and the local residents, who heretofore had managed quite nicely without any form of government, realized some form of civil authority was required to administer the estate. A meeting was held on February 17 in Champoeg and a probate judge appointed. The following day, another meeting was held, during which a constitutional committee was elected, as were several officers,

Jason Lee. *Public domain.*

one being high sheriff. The person taking this office was William Johnson, a Scotsman who had been in the employ of the HBC but now had a farm across the Willamette from Young's property.

By his own account, Johnson had served in the British navy, deserted, volunteered for the U.S. Navy and served aboard the USS *Constitution* during the War of 1812. After the war, he became a trapper, eventually finding his way to Fort Vancouver, where he joined the HBC (presumably not divulging his desertion from the British navy). Around 1835, he quit the company and built his cabin near the Willamette River. As high sheriff, his duties were probably not too onerous, given the still low number of residents in the area.

All this was about to change, for later in 1841 the first wagon train arrived via the Oregon Trail. There were fewer than one hundred in the party, but thousands more would be arriving in the coming years.

As for the issue of liquor sales to the natives, the absence of locally produced spirits was, in itself, not sufficient to eliminate the supply side of the equation. In 1842, the merchant ship *Blanche* arrived, carrying whiskey earmarked for trade with the natives. Efforts by the Methodist missionaries to block the exchange were not successful, and in the following drunkfest, three Chinook were shot and several more stabbed.[6]

The second wagon train arrived in September 1842, and among its members was Elijah White. He'd been busy back East conducting a smear campaign against Jason Lee and lobbying members of Congress to give him some official capacity in Oregon. He successfully passed himself off as an expert on Oregon and its affairs, largely because there was no one around to contradict him (it also helped that congressmen were no more clueful in 1841 than they are today). By offering to accept half wages, he was appointed "sub-Indian Agent" for Oregon and, having secured this, set about organizing a wagon train.

The party, numbering slightly more than one hundred, left Elm Grove, Missouri, on May 16, 1842. It wasn't long before the members became disenchanted with White's leadership and elected a new leader to replace him. Unfortunately, they let him remain with the party.

His return to Oregon was met with dismay by a number of residents, one of whom described White in her diary as a "self-important man."[7] Another described White as "not very bright; slow of perception."[8]

This observation was probably the result of White's claim that, as the only U.S. official in Oregon, he was the de facto "governor of the colony." No one but he took the claim seriously, and even his authority to act as Indian agent was called in to question on the entirely reasonable grounds that the U.S. government had no such prerogative in a territory it did not possess. The British position, as you might expect, was that White had no authority whatsoever.

Nevertheless, the Indians-with-liquor problem was considered serious enough that many were inclined to let White try to do something about it. The majority of whites residing in the area at this time had positive relationships with the natives, and the general feeling was "giving the Indians liquor will undermine their social structure, and that's a Bad Thing."

By April 1843, White had arrested eight individuals for selling liquor to the natives, with Sheriff Johnson presumably providing lodging for these in the Oregon City jail (White having no such facility of his own). Unfortunately, White's zealotry led him beyond the prosecution of those engaged in illicit trade with the natives, and he was soon persecuting people for the mere possession of spirits, even when intended for their own personal use. One such was Francis Pettygrove,[9] a man considered by the community to be "a merchant of good habits," whom White arrested for having brandy in his home. There was no legal basis for such an act, and those who understood this were gratified to see that White, like all bullies, would back down when confronted by someone who stood his or her ground. When he attempted to arrest an Englishwoman named Cooper for owning a barrel of whiskey, her forceful invocation of the authority of Great Britain likely caused White to realize Ms. Cooper's arrest would probably land him in the Fort Vancouver stockade. Later, when he boarded a ship belonging to John Couch intent on searching it for liquor, Couch and crew greeted him with "guns ranged fore and aft."[10] Even "slow of perception," White realized musket balls had far more authority than a scrap of paper from faraway Washington.

Elijah White. *Courtesy Oregon Historical Society, BB003858.*

Of course, I'm sure Dr. White was acting with good intentions, being unaware that the road to hell is paved with these and is well-worn by the tread of the self-righteous.

In the spring of 1843, White was called away to deal with disputes with tribes near

The Dalles. A number of significant events occurred during his absence.

The first was the reconvening of the provisional government on May 2, again at Champoeg. There had been no session in 1842, mostly because no one felt there was any need, but by 1843, the burgeoning population and a number of pressing issues convinced many that a greater degree of civil authority was needed, including, as historian Dr. Norman Clark wrote, "a governor, a judge, a jail, militia, and—some may have hoped—protection from Dr. White."[11] The details of the new government were worked out between May 16 and June 28, and the new "Organic Laws of Oregon" were formally adopted on July 5.

Joseph Meek. *Public domain.*

Joseph Meek, one of those most active in the creation of the new government, replaced William Johnson as sheriff. Johnson's departure from the position may well have been voluntary; he had sold his farm the year before, moving downriver to build a sawmill, and it might have been that the new enterprise demanded too much of his time. Nonetheless, his replacement by Joseph Meek might well have had unintended consequences.

Later in the year, James Conner, another ex-HBC employee, began operating a still near Oregon City, producing a concoction popularly known as "Blue Ruin." This was made from Hawaiian molasses with wheat and shorts thrown in for flavoring (shorts being a byproduct of flour production and consisting mostly of the fragmented outer husk of the wheat kernel). It was marketed to the natives as whiskey, but what Conner was producing was actually wheat-flavored rum because the absence of malt in the mash meant none of the wheat's starch could be converted to sugar.

Conner's operation was reported to White in January 1844. With ten volunteers assisting him, White was able to locate and destroy the still and then arrested Conner and fined him $300, a lot of money in those days (about $6,000 in 2016 dollars).

Undeterred, the following summer, Conner and his new partners, Richard McCrary and Hiram Straight, constructed another still and resumed the production of Blue Ruin. Again, White located and destroyed the still.

Enraged, Conner challenged White to a duel. Dueling being illegal (one of the legislature's latest laws), White promptly reported this to local authorities, and Conner was arrested. At his trial in October, he was convicted, fined $500 and disenfranchised for life.

Meanwhile, the provisional legislature was drafting a prohibition law. Passed on June 24, it banned the import, manufacture and sale of "ardent spirits," with a $100 fine for operating a distillery.[12] An exception to the sale proscription was made for physicians, who were allowed to sell "liquors as medicine, not to exceed one gallon at one time" (although with both import and production banned, one wonders how, exactly, a physician would obtain any spirits to sell).

It's important to understand this was not an all-encompassing prohibition of alcoholic beverages but only of distilled ("ardent") spirits. In an era when there was no safe supply of drinking water, banning beer, wine and hard cider would have been tantamount to condemning the population to death by dysentery. Everyone, even children, drank these beverages with their meals (Elijah White was a probable exception; it apparently was the case that microbial pathogens could not survive in his body).

The year ended on an interesting note; the legislature passed a law on December 23 "for the relief of James Conner":

> *That the fine assessed by the circuit court of Clackamas county at its October term, 1844, against James Conner, be and the same is hereby remitted; and that all the disabilities flowing from the judgment of said court be and the same are hereby removed, and that the said James Conner be restored to all the privileges of a citizen of Oregon.*[13]

This would appear to be the legislature's way of putting a lump of coal into Elijah White's Christmas stocking.

In 1845, during a visit to Fort Vancouver by the British warship *Modeste*, it became general knowledge that HBC kept a supply of rum on hand for the entertainment of Royal Navy officers and crew (the *Modeste* crew not being discreet in their enjoyment of the liquor). Subsequently, it became possible to tap into this supply, at least for those who knew the right person and had sufficient cash. Neither John McLoughlin nor his second-in-command, James Douglas, seemed able to do anything about this.

Nor could anyone slow the flow of Blue Ruin, which seemed more plentiful every day (rumor had it former sheriff Johnson had joined the ranks of the illicit distillers).

Furthermore, the attitude of the populace had shifted. With thousands of new settlers arriving every year, the views of Oregon's citizens began to mirror those of the United States as a whole, which were neither pro-temperance nor pro-Indian. Indeed, the general feeling was "giving the Indians liquor will undermine their social structure, and that's a Good Thing."

This change in sentiment was probably one factor in Elijah White's decision to resign his position as Indian agent in August 1845. He left for Washington, D.C, to petition Congress to reimburse him for expenses incurred during his tenure. The provisional legislature was happy to provide him with a resolution supporting this request (the subtext being *you sent him here, you pay him*).

At the end of 1846, the Oregon legislature repealed prohibition, replacing it with a licensing law. It did this in recognition of the current reality and sentiment and not, as later pro-temperance writers would claim, as the result of pressure by the "whiskey interests." Governor Abernathy vetoed the new law; however, support for it was strong, and there were more than enough votes to overturn the veto.

The new law set the annual license for selling hard liquor at $200 and for distilling it at $300, roughly equivalent to $4,000 and $6,000 in 2016 dollars, respectively. These were formidable sums and had been chosen in the hope that they would have a moderating effect on both the production and consumption of spirits.

The first license to sell spirits was obtained by Sidney Moss, who had built Oregon City's first hotel in 1844. Hardly a lowlife saloonkeeper, Moss was a founding member of the Oregon Lyceum Society and personally financed the first school in Oregon City.

In 1848, news of gold in California reached Oregon, and over half the adult male population left for the gold fields (the Oregon legislature was unable to meet that year because most of its members had done likewise). Because of its proximity to California, the Oregon contingent got many of the best claims, and a fair number returned with a good bit of gold in their packs. Investing in a liquor license seemed like a good way to put it to use, and soon Oregon City and Portland were dotted with saloons. Salem acquired its first in 1850, when successful gold digger Philip O'Reily opened his saloon, appropriately named the El Dorado.

The 1846 law also included strict prohibitions against the sale or distribution of liquor to the natives, with severe penalties for those who did. Despite this, Blue Ruin was still plentiful, and drunken natives often staggered into settlements singing Chinook drinking songs. Sidney Moss recorded one of these:

> *Nah! Six, potlatch blue lu.*
> *Nika ticky blue lu,*
> *Hiyu blue lu,*
> *Hyas olo,*
> *Potlatch blue lu.*

Roughly translated, it means:

> *Hello! Friend, throw a party, give me whiskey.*
> *I want whiskey,*
> *Plenty of whiskey,*
> *Very thirsty,*
> *Throw a party, give me whiskey.*

Indeed, the potlatch, traditionally a banquet-format party with much mutual gift-giving, was rapidly devolving into nothing more than a binge-drinking event.

Sheriff Meek pursued the makers and dispensers of Blue Ruin with vigor and in 1846 arrested former sheriff William Johnson for selling spirits to the natives. Of course, for every one arrested, another took his place; in that same year, an individual named O'Brian (first name unknown) is reported to have also begun illicit distilling operations.

William Johnson was not long out of commission because we know he was back at it again the following year. Some years later, his partner in crime, Edouard Chambreau, described an 1847 transaction:

> *The next morning the skiff [boat] was made ready with a 20 gallon keg of Blue Ruin. This was hid [sic] under the things in the bottom of the boat. There were quite a number of Indians camped here, and they were anxious to "swap for lumm."*
>
> *We made them sit down in rows with their different things they had to put their Lumm in, and whatever they had to pay for it. They were all on the beach about ten steps from the skiff. We went to every one*

before we began to pour it out in their vessels, and agreed on what should be given for this and that measure full. Having done this, Johnson began to pour out and I carried the things to the boat. The principle things we got in exchange was Beaver and Otter skins, and Hudson's Bay blankets.

An Indian, when he drinks whisky, he will drink as long as he can hold his breath. By the time he [Johnson] *was getting through with the last ones, the first ones were getting very funny. He shouted to me to run for the boat. I ran to the boat and shoved it until I was knee deep in the water. As he had the whisky, some of them followed him to the boat. He was retreating backwards with his keg under his arm and his long knife in the other. In the meantime, I covered him with my rifle. Before it takes time to tell it, he threw the keg with what remained in it as far as he could toward the camp. This gave him a chance to get away from those who were immediately near him, and he got into the boat.*

We were almost in swimming water, with three Indians hanging yet to the boat. We knocked them over the head and shoved off just in the nick of time, because we had no more than had them loose from the boat than there was a gang of about 30 that came running and yelling with all their might. Then the fighting was among themselves.

On this trip we made very near $500 apiece. The reader can draw his own conclusions of what must have been the scene in that Indian camp with 20 gallons of that abominable stuff in them.[14]

Johnson died the following year, at age fifty-eight. The creek next to which he built his sawmill is still known as Johnson's Creek.

His partner, Edouard Chambreau, continued his life of misadventure until 1874, when repeated visits by pro-temperance ladies to his Portland saloon led to a moral turnaround (we'll learn more about these ladies in chapter 6). He sold his interest in the saloon and, the following year, volunteered as a scout for the U.S. Army. In 1880, he returned to Portland to start a grocery business. He died in 1902 at age eighty-one.

James Conner probably continued his moonshining ways. He appears in the 1850 Oregon territorial census, listed as a farmer living in Polk County. There are no later records of him or his activities.

As mentioned earlier, Ewing Young died in 1841, at forty-two years of age. An elementary school in Newberg, Oregon, is named after him.

John McLoughlin, who had become progressively more pro-American during the 1840s, resigned his position with the Hudson's Bay Company in 1846. He moved his family to Oregon City and opened a general store. He became an American citizen in 1849 and died in 1857. No fewer than four schools are named after him (two in Washington and two in Oregon), along with a bridge in Portland and a mountain in southern Oregon. A statue of McLoughlin stands on the capitol grounds in Salem.

Joseph Meek became a federal marshal after Oregon became part of the United States in 1848. He died in 1875 at age sixty-five.

Sidney Moss continued as a prosperous businessman in Oregon City. In 1878, he published *Pictures of Pioneer Times at Oregon City*. He died in 1901.

Jason Lee returned to New York in 1844 to answer the charges made by Elijah White. He succeeded in refuting White's claims, but the effort destroyed his health. He died on March 12, 1845, at age forty-one. In 1906, his remains were brought back to Oregon and buried in the old mission cemetery. A statue of Lee sits on the capitol grounds in Salem, facing the one of McLoughlin.

Elijah White received his requested compensation from Congress. In 1850, he was in Washington Territory, promoting the community of Pacific City and selling property to settlers. In 1861, he moved to California, where he died a wealthy man in 1879.

Blue Ruin Wallbanger

½ tablespoon Ottis Webber Oregon Wheat Whiskey
1½ ounces light Oregon rum
3 ounces orange juice
½ ounce Galliano

Shake whiskey, rum and juice with ice; strain into a chilled glass. Top with Galliano.

3

SUNSHINE

he first licensed distiller in Oregon was John Anderson, a Swedish immigrant living in Clackamas County. Sidney Moss reports his first purchase of locally produced whiskey was from a "John Anderson of Salem," for which he paid six dollars per gallon in 1847.[15] Anderson's farm was south of Molalla, close to the Marion county line and about fifteen miles northeast of Salem, and probably because Anderson was shipping downriver from this city, Moss describes him as "of Salem."

In the 1850 census (as well as those following), Anderson lists his occupation as "farmer," and apart from Moss's statement, there are no other records of Anderson's distilling activities. This suggests whiskey production was a sideline operation, perhaps one conducted during the winter, using surplus grain from the autumn harvest.

From what was Anderson making his whiskey? At the time, the preeminent grain (in fact, the preeminent crop) in the Willamette Valley was wheat. Barley was a distant second, followed by oats and corn (rye is not mentioned in any accounts of the period). It thus seems plausible Anderson's whiskey was made mostly from wheat, with some malted barley thrown in to facilitate starch-to-sugar conversion.

The first commercial distillery in Oregon was started by William Bowman. Originally from North Carolina, Bowman arrived in 1844 and settled in the now extinct Polk County town of O'Neil's Mill (later known as Ellendale),[16] filing a land claim on January 7, 1846. The community was founded by James O'Neil, who'd been with Ewing Young on the 1837 cattle drive from

California. Located on the Siskiyou Trail, the gristmill built by O'Neil during the winter of 1844–45 was the only one in Oregon south of Oregon City and was used by farmers from all over the Willamette Valley.

To date, I've found only one reference to Bowman's operation: a single paragraph in a 1911 article, "The Story of Ellendale" by Claud Shaw:[17]

> *While O'Neil was operating his mill, his future father-in-law, Mr. Bowman, built near the mill the first whisky distillery ever erected in Oregon. He had journeyed across the plains in 1844, and owing to his constant use of the term as a by-work, was known to everyone as "Jularker" Bowman [jularker* is a southern Appalachian term roughly translating to "roguish beau"; think Rhett Butler]. *In making his liquor, he used wheat. This established another small market for the farmer; gave additional distinction to the place, and filled the purse of "Jularker" Bowman. To accommodate the patrons of the mill and distillery, he also conducted a private hotel.*

In fact, the "hotel" (more of a country inn with a small store on the premises) was owned by O'Neil; Bowman managed ("conducted") it for him. In 1849, O'Neil sold the mill and inn to James Nesmith. The mill and

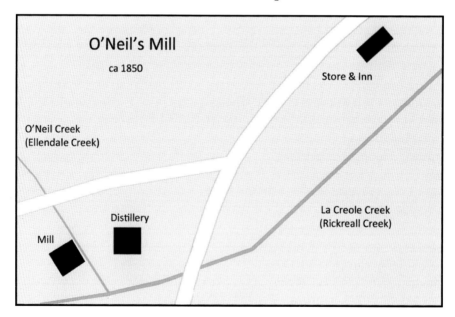

O'Neil's Mill (Ellendale) circa 1850. *Map by the author.*

Second store and inn structure at O'Neil's Mill, built in 1861. *Photo by the author.*

inn continued to operate for many years thereafter. The latter was destroyed by fire in 1860; the replacement structure, built in 1861, still stands and is now a private residence.

Examination of license fees paid to the provisional government's treasury during the late 1840s suggests Bowman's license was probably granted in 1848.

I imagine Bowman's whiskey was pretty rough, having spent little (if any) time in a barrel, but to the patrons of O'Neil's mill, most of whom had spent several days driving a wagonload of grain to the site, it probably tasted pretty good. Sitting behind the inn, sipping Bowman's whiskey and watching the waters of La Creole Creek (now known as Rickreall Creek) flow by was as good a way as any to spend one's time while waiting for your grain to be ground.

William Bowman died in 1851, and it seems the distilling operation did not survive him. Bowman's daughter Tabitha married James O'Neil in 1855 (Shaw's description of Bowman as O'Neil's "future father-in-law" prompts the question: can you be someone's father-in-law if they didn't marry your daughter until *after* you died?). When Bowman's widow, Sarah Bowman, died in 1861, O'Neil purchased the Bowman farm from William's son.

Over the course of the 1850s, Willamette agriculture began to diversify. With abundant winter rain complemented by abundant summer sunshine, nearly any temperate region crop flourished there. As described in chapter 2, the staff at Fort Vancouver had great success with a variety of grains and with apple and pear trees. Cultivation of fruit received a major boost in 1847 when Henderson Luelling arrived with over seven hundred one-year-old grafted fruit and nut trees, which included eighteen varieties of apples, eight varieties of pears, six varieties of cherries, and three types of peaches, as well as quince, black walnut, shell-bark hickory, grape, currant and gooseberry plants.[18]

Luelling's apple trees began bearing fruit in 1851, and two years later, he shipped four bushels of apples to San Francisco. He sold numerous young trees to local famers, and by 1861, seventy-five thousand bushels were exported from Oregon.[19]

Much of the apple crop was consumed locally, and a large percentage was made into hard cider, a beverage that, at least in rural areas, was more widely consumed than beer. With apples being so plentiful, by the end of the 1850s the typical Oregon farmer-distiller was producing apple brandy (applejack) rather than whiskey.

Again, most of this was consumed quite young, having spent little or no time in a barrel. It was also consumed locally, there being little demand for it in Portland and Oregon City. These cities were served by ships arriving from the eastern United States and other locations, and their cargos included whiskey, rum and brandy. In fact, examination of Sidney Moss's ledgers from this period shows that although he was getting his whiskey from a local producer, he was buying rum and brandy from merchants in Portland and Oregon City (said examination also revealed Moss had extremely bad handwriting).

There being plenty of demand for these products, many of those importing them became quite wealthy. One such was William Ladd, who arrived in 1851 with a cargo of wine and liquor, established a residence in Portland and continued to import these products. Ladd reinvested his profits in numerous enterprises in the Portland area and built a large estate in the 1870s. The carriage house, built in 1883, survives and is today the Raven & Rose restaurant.

Consequently, anyone wanting to establish a commercial distillery of any size needed to do it in a location where transport from Portland incurred an uncompetitive premium.

One such place was the upper (southern) end of the Willamette Valley, where in 1846 Eugene Skinner established a farm. The community that grew up around him was originally known as Skinner's Mudhole but was renamed Eugene City in 1850. In 1851, an enterprising individual named Hillyard Shaw dug a millrace there along the west bank of the Willamette River and constructed a sawmill the following year. In 1856, a gristmill was completed, a boon to southern Willamette farmers who now no longer needed to haul their grain all the way to O'Neil's Mill.

The next enterprise to establish itself along the millrace was **Eugene City Distilling Company**, which was in operation before the end of 1856. There isn't much information available about the company, such as the identity of its owners or from what grain it made its whiskey (though it's likely it was mostly wheat). The longest reference to it found to date is a passage in Albert Walling's 1884 *An Illustrated History of Lane County*:

> *We find that the internal revenue tax on spirits manufactured at Eugene City distillery at this period, amounted to about nine hundred dollars per month or ten thousand dollars a year. Besides, the license for the distillery was one thousand six hundred dollars per annum, so that the total tax paid by the Eugene City Distilling Company amounted to nearly twelve thousand dollars annually, or as much as the whole amount of revenue collected in the county from all other sources. They were at this time manufacturing in the vicinity of seventy gallons of whisky daily or one thousand eight hundred gallons per month, an average that could have been kept up each month of the year. This industry, which was situated on the bank of the river in the northeast portion of the town, contained all the latest improvements and manufactured a first-class article.*[20]

"This period" was 1869, which, based on IRS data, was in fact the peak production year for the distillery; in most years it was less. Nevertheless, the daily output capability of seventy gallons of one-hundred-proof whiskey was a lot for a town with only 200 residents in 1856 and only 861 in 1870, and it's reasonable to assume the distillery was supplying most of the upper valley's demand.

After producing about 7,600 gallons of whiskey during fiscal year 1870 (July 1, 1869, to June 30, 1870), the distillery ceased operations. No mention is made of the event in the *Guard*, Eugene's only newspaper of the period (which is itself something of a mystery, given the distillery's status as the county's foremost taxpayer).

The distillery's demise is probably the result of improved transportation technologies that occurred over the course of the 1860s. At the start of the decade, most merchant ships were sailing vessels, and bringing one of these around stormy Cape Horn was a challenge. Within the Willamette Valley itself, the only transportation from Portland to Eugene was by wagon road or by rowed flatboat. Large steamships could not cross the Willamette Falls at Oregon City until locks were built in 1873.

The situation began to change during the second half of the 1860s. Many of the sailing ships in the U.S. merchant fleet had been destroyed by Confederate cruisers during the Civil War, and in the building boom following the war, most of the new ships were steam powered. It was a lot easier for a three-thousand-ton iron-hulled steamship to get around Cape Horn than it was for a one-thousand-ton wooden sailing ship, and the volume of cargo reaching West Coast ports increased commensurately.

On the Willamette itself, steamships were constructed and launched above Willamette Falls at about this same time, with the *Echo* reaching Eugene in 1865. These were smaller ships than those operating on the lower Willamette and on the Columbia, but they still carried a useful load (the *Echo*'s capacity was a little over one hundred tons).[21]

Then there were the railroads. The first transcontinental route was completed in 1869, and goods reaching San Francisco by rail could be loaded onto coastal steamers and transported to Portland. In Oregon, the Oregon Central Railroad (which later became the Oregon & California Railroad) began construction of a line along the Willamette in 1868, reaching Albany in 1870, Eugene in 1871 and Roseburg in 1872. Construction ceased the following year because of a stock market crash and the ensuing depression.[22]

With all these transportation improvements, spirits produced in the eastern United States and elsewhere could now reach the upper Willamette Valley and be sold at a competitive price, and in the September 17, 1870 issue of the *Guard*, there was a promotional blurb for its new advertiser, the E. Miller Company. The advertisement itself, which occupied a full column of the paper, offered not only two popular brands of Kentucky Bourbon but also gin from England, rum from Jamaica and, for the well-heeled, Hennessy and Martell Cognac from France. Fine wines were available, too, including champagne from Piper-Heidsieck and Veuve Clicquot Ponsardin (yes, folks, Skinner's Mudhole had *arrived*).

I believe the local distillery's shutdown at this same point in time was more than coincidence. Although Walling, fourteen years later, described the distillery's product as "a first-class article," the owners probably recognized their wheat whiskey was not "first-class" at all, and decided it was time to call it quits.

Another location well removed from the docks in Portland was the Rogue Valley in the southwest part of the state. Gold was discovered here in 1851, and the area was soon swarming with miners seeking to extract it from the ground, along with those seeking to extract it from the miners by supplying them with the necessities of life—bread, meat, eggs, beer and whiskey.

In 1854, two flouring mills were established, **Ashland Mills** (around which the city of Ashland grew) and, to the northwest of this, on Bear Creek, **Eagle Mills**. The latter, owned by two brothers, Michael and Tobias Thomas, soon expanded its operations to include brewing and distilling. The first known reference to the distilling operation was an advertisement that appeared in the February 6, 1858 issue of the Jacksonville newspaper the *Oregon Sentinel.*

> *EAGLE MILLS.*
>
> *THE subscribers now having their Mill and Distillery in excellent repair, would respectfully inform their patrons and the public generally that they are now prepared to do all kinds of Merchant Mill business, and are also furnishing a choice lot of Liquors, consisting of Gin, Brandy, Whisky, Lager Beer, &c.*
>
> *THOMAS & JACOBS.*
> *Eagle Mills, Jan. 23, 1858*

Jacobs was Joseph Jacobs, the mill's bookkeeper and sales agent.

The 1860 census shows, among those housed on the mill property, a brewer, Edward Harp (born in Germany in 1821), and a distiller, Joseph Chaffee (born in Pennsylvania in 1818). The census also shows Tobias Thomas and his family lived adjacent to the mill operation. It's not known where elder brother Michael lived; it's entirely possible, based on census information, he didn't even live in Oregon.

The Thomas brothers evidently had trouble meeting their financial obligations, because in June 1861, their mortgage holder, Allen Farnham, filed for foreclosure on the Eagle Mills property. In February 1862, the Circuit Court of Jackson County awarded the property to Farnham, which consisted of:

> *Ten acres of land, together with the Eagle Mills, store house, blacksmith shop, distillery, the right of way to the tail race from the Eagle Mill to where*

it terminates in Bear creek, with fifteen feet on each side of said tail race; the right and interest obtained from William Newhouse for constructing a dam and race to turn the water from Bear creek to Eagle Mill—with all the improvements, appurtenances [an accessory or other item associated with a particular activity] *and hereditaments* [anything which can be passed by an individual to heirs] *belonging to the same.*

Farnham had been in the area for less than a year, having recently arrived from Massachusetts. It's not known how he acquired the mill property mortgage. Perhaps he arrived with money in his pockets or made a good strike in the gold fields.

We know Farnham continued the distilling operations until at least early 1864 because advertisements in the *Sentinel* continue to give the company's name as "**Eagle Distillery and Flour Mill**" (these advertisements show Farnham retained Joseph Jacobs, which suggests the Thomas brothers' problems were not due to faulty bookkeeping or representation). However, advertisements from 1865 and later make no mention of the distillery operation, and IRS tax rolls from the latter part of the decade record no distilling activity at the site.

This absence from the tax rolls may well provide a clue. Although the federal government normally received sufficient operating funds from custom tariffs, the debts incurred by warfare required supplemental income, and the excise tax on distilled spirits was the go-to option for this. George Washington, seeking to pay off the Revolutionary War debt, was the first to impose this tax, which led to the famous "Whiskey Rebellion" by the farmer-distillers of Pennsylvania (which, by the way, did not play out exactly the way it's usually described in the history books, but then, did anything happen exactly the way it's described in the history books?).

The tax was repealed in 1802 but then reinstated in 1812 to pay for the War of 1812 and not repealed again until 1834 (much of Washington had to be rebuilt, having been burned by the British in 1814).

In 1861, the nation embarked on its most expensive war to date, this being the one it was fighting with itself. In 1862, the excise tax on spirits production was reinstated, along with an income tax (later declared unconstitutional), taxes on the ownership of various items (such as horses, gold watches, silver-plate) as well as occupational licenses for nearly every occupation other than farmer (the fee for these occupational licenses varied by profession; the cost of being a juggler was higher than for being a lawyer, *which is just wrong*).

Along with the spirits excise tax came the machinery required to enforce it: "gaugers" (IRS agents who measured and recorded the quantities of spirits produced and barreled), "bonded" warehouses (locations, usually at the distillery itself, where spirits were stored) and "storekeepers" (IRS agents who administered the bonded warehouses).

Examination of IRS annual reports for fiscal years 1863, 1864 and 1865 shows both enforcement and compliance were considerably less than optimum. Indeed, in his preface to the 1866 report, IRS commissioner Edward Rollins lamented, "There is probably no tax imposed by the law which is so largely evaded by those subject to its provision as the tax upon distilled spirits."

The tax rate started at the modest level of twenty cents per proof gallon (50 percent ABV) but had reached two dollars per gallon by 1865. The rates up to 1917 can be found in the following table.

FROM	TO	RATE
August 1, 1862	March 7, 1864	0.20
March 7, 1864	July 1, 1864	0.60
July 1, 1864	January 1, 1865	1.50 0.50 grape brandy
January 1, 1865	July 20, 1868	2.00 0.50 grape brandy until July 1866 1.50 apple and peach brandy until July 1866
July 20, 1868	June 6, 1872	0.50
June 6, 1872	March 3, 1875	0.70
March 3, 1875	August 27, 1894	0.90
August 27, 1894	October 3, 1917	1.10

The 1860s' rising tax rate, along with more efficient enforcement, had the effect of squeezing out most of the farmer-distillers, who had probably exceeded twenty in number in Oregon by 1863. Their operations were small scale, usually producing fewer than two hundred gallons per year, using small stills they either made themselves or purchased for a moderate price.[23]

As mentioned above, Eagle Mills stopped advertising its distilled and brewed products in mid-1864, the same time the excise tax increased from $0.60 to $1.50. I suspect Allen Farnham felt his profit margin was too low to afford the tax increase (it might also be he didn't like the idea of IRS inspectors looking over his shoulder).

Most of the IRS tax rolls from the nineteenth century have not survived, but there are a number available from 1867 to 1873 for Oregon (unfortunately, not a complete set). These provide a useful window onto the distilling operations of the period.

In 1867, in addition to the Eugene City Distilling Company, we find three additional commercial distilleries. The **Corvallis Brewing Company** was founded in 1861 by George Bauerlin (born in 1823), originally from Germany but lately arrived from Portland. Bauerlin operated the brewery himself until 1866, but on the Saturday night of June 15 the "very much intoxicated" Bauerlin became involved in a brawl at a downtown Corvallis saloon. Having received a severe beating by two individuals (James Woody and James Herron), he staggered off in the general direction of the Willamette River. Those familiar with the Corvallis riverfront can tell you it's a bit of a drop, and Bauerlin's body was found on the riverbank on Sunday. Two local doctors examined the body and pronounced the cause of death as drowning but expressed the belief "that the wounds found upon the body of the deceased were such as might ultimately have caused death." Woody and Herron were subsequently arrested.[24]

Mrs. Bauerlin leased the brewery to another German family, the Hunts. The family patriarch was Bernard Hunt, and he and son Joseph had opened Hunt's Lager Beer Saloon in Corvallis sometime in the early 1860s.

The tax rolls from the late 1860s show, in addition to brewing beer and hard cider, the Hunts were making modest quantities of applejack (about twenty to twenty-five gallons per month).

The Hunt family's fortunes took a turn for the worse in 1869, when a fire in Corvallis destroyed several city blocks, including the one where their saloon was located. The following year, in April, the brewery/distillery building itself was destroyed by fire. The building was insured for $3,800; however, this did not cover the losses, and the Bauerlins decided to not rebuild.

Joseph Hunt eventually built a brewery of his own, but its history was short and troubled (it was briefly seized by the IRS in 1870).[25] There is no record of any distilling taking place at the new brewery.

Down in Roseburg, **Mehl & Rast**, the brewery started in the early 1860s by Gottlieb Mehl (German) and John Rast (Swiss), was also producing apple and peach brandy, with monthly output ranging from forty to seventy gallons. An advertisement appearing in the April 30, 1867 edition of the *Roseburg Ensign* offered "Lager Beer, Apple Brandy, Peach Brandy, Whiskey, Cider,

Etc., Etc." It's not known how long the company was distilling, Oregon tax rolls after 1868 being incomplete or nonexistent, but I suspect it ceased soon after the railroad reached Roseburg in 1872. The brewery (sold by Mehl's widow to Max Weiss in 1898) continued to turn out fifteen barrels per day of "Roseburger Export Beer" up until Prohibition, after which it became an ice plant (the brewery had gotten into the ice business during the 1890s).

Returning to Jackson County, we find apple and peach brandy being produced by Joseph Wetterer of Jacksonville. Another German, Wetterer arrived in the area during the late 1850s and purchased the Eagle Saloon and Brewery in 1859 from its original owner, J.J. Holman. From 1859 until mid-1864, his advertisements referenced the business as "Eagle Brewery," but commencing in mid-1865, this changed to **"Eagle Brewery and Distillery**." This is so close in distance (twelve miles) and time (twelve months) to the "Eagle Distillery and Flour Mill" that it's reasonable to believe there was a transfer of both the distilling equipment and the trademark for the name "Eagle Distillery" from one company to the other. Unfortunately, there are no surviving records supporting this scenario.

EAGLE BREWERY
-AND-
DISTILLERY

JOSEPH WETTERER has now on hand, and is constantly manufacturing FINE WHISKEY, BRANDIES and LAGER BEER, which he will sell in quantities from one quart to one barrel and upwards, to suit purchasers. Call and test his Liquors.

Jacksonville, March 3d, 1865.

Wetterer's business was located near the center of Jacksonville, at 355 South Oregon Street. The first structure built at the location, in 1856, was a combined saloon and office, with the brewery/distillery being located in an adjoining structure behind the saloon. After Wetterer acquired the property in 1859, he built a home next to the saloon for himself and his family.

IRS records from 1867 and later show Wetterer producing only fruit brandy. However, his own advertisements state he was producing whiskey, and the February 11, 1882 edition of the *Sentinel* reported Peter Berwert, an employee at Wetterer's distillery, was injured while using a candle to inspect the contents of a whiskey barrel (I suspect this was Berwert's first and last day on the job). Wetterer was either making whiskey only occasionally or was simply not reporting it to the IRS (review of IRS annual reports found no explicit statement that fruit distillers were subject to less scrutiny than whiskey distillers, but "reading between the lines" gives one the impression this was the case; Wetterer may well have been taking advantage of this).

Joseph Wetterer died in July 1879. Widow Frederika continued with the operation for a number of years; there is mention in the April 7, 1883 *Sentinel* that she'd hired a new brewer from San Francisco. In June of the same year, she remarried to a William Heeley and probably ceased production that year as well.

She still had stocks of beer and whiskey and continued to advertise these until March 1884.

Liquor House.

The undersigned offers Whiskey for sale in quantities to suit customers at $3 per gallon or $1 per quart, at the Eagle Brewery. Lager Beer for sale and delivered at the usual price.

Mrs. J. Wetterer.

Wetterer residence is at left, Eagle Saloon at right. The brewery/distillery was located behind the saloon. *Courtesy Southern Oregon Historical Society.*

Returning to the tax rolls from 1867, we find a number of farmer-distillers persisting with brandy production despite the excise tax having risen to two dollars per gallon. Making applejack were Thomas Standley of Yamhill County; John Settle and Dayton Simison of Linn County; Claiborne Neil of Jackson County; and William Avery, John Hug and Edward Mathiot of Marion County.

The last two, who both lived near the now extinct community of Butteville, merit some additional mention. John Hug was a Swiss immigrant who, in 1852, came west with three other men of Swiss origin. One of these was Peter Britt, a photographer with about three hundred pounds of photographic equipment in his baggage. When the group reached the Grande Ronde Valley, two of the party announced they weren't willing to haul Britt's equipment any farther. Hug, a wagon maker by trade, was able to reconstruct the party's large single wagon into two smaller ones, one for he and Britt and one for the other two members of the party, who trekked on ahead and, once reaching the Columbia River, built a raft and made it to Portland in only twenty-four hours (which had to be a wild ride). Hug and Britt continued on the overland route, eventually reaching Portland some days later. From there, they proceeded south, with Hug settling in Champoeg and resuming his career as a wagon maker, and Britt continuing down to Jacksonville and starting a photography business. By the mid-1860s, Hug had acquired a farm and a family and was converting a portion of his apple crop into cider and applejack.

Edward Mathiot was a Frenchman (born in 1837) who came to Oregon in 1853 with his parents and six siblings.[26] IRS tax rolls from 1867 show he was making brandy from grapes as well as from apples. This distinguishes him as one of the first viticulturists in the Willamette Valley, as well as probably being the first producer of grape brandy in the state of Oregon.

Tax rolls subsequent to 1868 are incomplete, but even so, it's pretty clear the number of Oregon farmer-distillers was declining.

From 1868 to 1873 the IRS annual report showed the excise tax, by state, generated by spirits produced from various sources and separated grape brandy from that made from apples or peaches. From this dollar value, you can compute the number of gallons produced. For Oregon's, see the table on page 50.

From this data it appears the autumn of 1869 was the last time Edward Mathiot produced grape brandy (fiscal year 1870 ran from July 1, 1869, to June 30, 1870).

DISTILLED IN OREGON

Fiscal Year	Grape Brandy (in gallons)	Apple and Peach Brandy (in gallons)
1868	120	539
1869	0	625
1870	118	548
1871	0	344
1872	0	1,575

The 1872 production spike can be attributed to a commercial distillery, G.A. Crawford & Co. of Clackamas County. The company was apparently in business for only a year because in 1873, statewide brandy production was back down to 514 gallons.

Commencing in 1873, the IRS annual report listed the number registered and operating distilleries by state, as well as the excise tax generated by these (again, from this value you can compute the number of gallons produced). Unfortunately, it also started combining the data for grape brandy with those for apple and peach, a practice it continued through 1888.

What can we deduce from the figures in the following table?

Fiscal Year	Distilleries Registered	Distilleries Operating	Gallons
1873	3	3	514
1874	3	3	503
1875	4	3	585
1876	2	2	112
1877	3	3	703
1878	4	4	1,407
1879	8	8	1,355
1880	9	9	1,565
1881	9	9	1,294
1882	8	8	1,747
1883	5	5	1,141
1884	4	4	358
1885	5	5	814
1886	10	10	2,688
1887	11	11	2,353
1888	7	7	780

First, it's pretty clear from 1878 through 1883, there was a distillery producing around 50 to 60 percent of the state's total output. Unfortunately, efforts to identify this distillery haven't borne fruit.

In 1886, there's a doubling of the number of distilleries, but a 330 percent increase in production. The fact that 1888's return to 1885 levels suggest no more than four distilleries (and possibly as few as one) were responsible for this dramatic increase.

Finally, we should recognize this wasn't a lot of brandy. In the peak production year of 1886, Oregon's population was about 250,000; even if only 20 percent of the population drank alcohol, this would have provided only about seven ounces per person.

So where were Oregonians getting their liquor? Then, as now, most of it was imported. Data for total sales is not available, but the IRS required wholesalers to report their inventory each October 1, and these figures give some idea of the relative quantities of liquor being brought into the state.

The list below shows the inventories reported by Oregon wholesalers on October 1, 1879.

Spirit Type	Gallons
bourbon	25,053
rye whiskey	1,909
Irish whiskey	0
Scotch whisky	409
New England rum	479
Jamaica rum	79
St. Croix rum	0
gin	3,175
Holland gin	159
neutral	1,956
miscellaneous	3,604

Clearly, bourbon was the spirit-of-choice among imbibing Oregonians, and this probably explains why locally produced wheat whiskey was uncompetitive.

A distant second is "Miscellaneous." I suspect this was mostly grape brandy, with California product comprising a larger percentage than French.

Gin is the third most popular. Most was probably London dry style, but another popular type of the period was Old Tom, a softer style sweetened with sugar.

Again, this is a snapshot of what was in inventory; the actual annual quantities sold and consumed were multiples of these figures, possibly ten times as much.

In addition to the imported and legally produced local spirits, there was certainly some quantity produced illicitly. Just because it became legal to operate a licensed distillery in 1847 doesn't mean all who wanted to produce spirit were willing to pay the license fee, much less the excise taxes that kicked in during the 1860s. As we've seen, there were many producing moonshine in the 1840s, and there's no reason to believe this activity simply stopped. Estimating the quantities produced, however, is nearly impossible.

Commencing in the 1877 annual report, the IRS began publishing a count of illegal stills found and seized or destroyed. The figures through 1900 can be found on the table on page 53.

The number seized in Oregon seems astonishingly low, but before reading too much into the figure, it makes sense to adjust the expected number relative to Oregon's percentage of the overall population of the United States. In 1880, the state's population was .35 percent of the U.S. total; in 1890, it was .5 percent; and in 1900, it was .54 percent. Assuming 1) an equal percentage of Oregonians were operating illicit stills as in the rest of the country, and 2) IRS agents in the state were as effective as elsewhere, then the number of stills seized by the IRS in Oregon during this period should have been around 115, or 112 more than the reported number.

So the discrepancy is rather astonishing and suggests either almost no one in Oregon was operating illegal stills or that local IRS agents were almost totally ineffective in their search-and-destroy efforts.

The first proposition seems unlikely. There was definitely a market for liquor, and although there was plenty of legal spirit available (both locally produced and imported), the price of this was inflated by licensing fees and excise taxes; most likely there were many who didn't want to spend the extra money if they could avoid it. Nor can it be argued that most Oregonians of the time were particularly law-abiding, especially if those laws originated in faraway Washington, D.C. Anyone who's studied the history of the state knows Oregon was, in the latter half of the nineteenth century, probably the most "southern" of the non-seceding states, having many Confederate sympathizers during the Civil War and an ardently anti-federal attitude during the Reconstruction period when Congress was under the control of the so-called Radical Republicans. So I think it's a safe assumption there were as many illicit stills operating in Oregon (percentage wise) as elsewhere in the nation (if you don't find this argument persuasive, I'd like to introduce you to my acquaintance Dr. Ghitmi Mobouti).[27]

Year	National Total	Oregon Total
1877	598	0
1878	1,020	0
1879	1,319	0
1880	969	0
1881	756	0
1882	464	0
1883	397	0
1884	377	0
1885	245	0
1886	564	3
1887	456	0
1888	518	0
1889	466	0
1890	583	0
1891	795	0
1892	852	0
1893	806	0
1894	1,016	0
1895	1,874	0
1896	1,905	0
1897	2,273	0
1898	2,391	0
1899	2,190	0
1900	1,955	0
Total	24,789	3

It's far more likely the Oregon branch of the IRS, in its efforts to locate illicit stills, simply received little or no help from the local populace. Inquiries about moonshining operations were met with blank stares and replies of feigned ignorance.

The state's geography was probably also a factor. Mountains, hidden valleys and dense forests made search-and-destroy missions extremely challenging and ultimately unsuccessful.

So trying to quantify the amount of illicitly produced spirit in late nineteenth-century Oregon is impossible, the best estimate being probably a lot.

Of course, there were those who preferred to distill legally, and if located in a sufficiently populated area beyond the reach of railroads and riverboats, it was possible to do so and turn a profit. One such area was the Rogue River Valley, which continued to have a fair number of miners, along with farmers and townspeople. The railroad had made it no farther south than Roseburg before the financial collapse of 1872, and the Rogue River itself was not even remotely navigable for riverboats. So the area had a number of successful distillers during the 1870s.

We've already met Joseph and Frederika Wetterer of Jacksonville, whose enterprise ended sometime around 1882. Supplementing their production was that of several other local commercial producers.

Joseph Hockett, born in 1845 in Iowa, arrived in the area in 1877 with wife Sarah and five children (including the one-year-old twins, Maud and Claud). They settled in the community of Phoenix (about three miles southeast of present-day Medford), where Hockett started the Phoenix Distillery and Saloon. The Jacksonville paper, the *Oregon Sentinel*, reported in its November 20, 1878 edition, "The distillery and saloon owned by Hockett & Smith, is doing a good business, and supplies a superior quality of apple-jack and lager beer."

For the next two years, Hockett frequently ran an advertisement in the *Sentinel*:

PHOENIX DISTILLERY
AND SALOON
Phoenix, - - - -   Ogn.

THE UNDERSIGNED HAS TAKEN full charge of this business and is prepared to furnish the public with a first-class quality of Brandy, Wine and Cider. The saloon will always be supplied with the best of liquors and cigars. Oysters and sardines always kept on hand.

J.L. HOCKETT

In the February 11, 1880 edition there appeared two rather strange articles in the *Sentinel*. The first read:

Oscar Kilbourne, U.S. Gauger, is among us on official business. On Monday he visited the distillers at Phoenix and will attend to business here until Friday. He is accompanied by Edward Hall, manager of the

Imperial, London, Northern and Queen Fire Insurance Co. This fact creates a suspicion of the "fiery" character of Jackson county whiskey which needs explanation.

This sounds alarming, but was probably only an attempt at humor, because there is no subsequent report of arrest or fine being imposed on Hockett, and he continued to advertise for most of the next year.

Nevertheless, for reasons unknown, in September 1881, Hockett sold the business to Thomas Pankey, a local farmer. There are no subsequent reports of the Phoenix distillery, and I suspect Pankey purchased it because he wanted the property, not the business.

The other article of interest was this: "TOMATO BRANDY—Among the packages gauged by Mr. Kilbourne at Neff's distillery on Wagner Creek, was a barrel of brandy made from tomatoes."

This teasing tidbit was followed by a longer article on March 31:

TOMATO BRANDY—In February last we noticed the gauging of a barrel of tomato brandy at Neff's distillery, by U.S. Gauger Kilbourne. On Monday a sample was brought to Jacksonville by Mr. Neff, and it is really a fine flavored article but, of course, lacking age. It is 100 proof and a delicate tomato flavor can be detected. An enquiry about this brandy has been received from a wholesale liquor dealer in Philadelphia, as it is the finest that has been made from tomatoes. It takes four bushels of fruit for a gallon of brandy which is worth $6.

I've no doubt this was the "finest [brandy] that has been made from tomatoes" because I suspect it was the *only* brandy ever made from tomatoes. Checking Amy Stewart's *The Drunken Botanist*, which lists an astonishing variety of foods from which humans have produced liquor, I find no mention of tomato-based spirit.

The distiller of the tomato spirit, Thomas Neff, was a Virginian who'd arrived in the area during the 1870s with wife Mary and young son Jesse. Neff was, in fact, a Confederate veteran, who later in life was quoted as saying he believed he'd been on the wrong side. The 1880 census finds him in the Eden district of the county, which was located between Medford and Phoenix, and records his occupation as "distiller." References to his distillery describe it as being located on Wagner Creek, the terminal end of which is about four miles southeast of the Eden area.

Thirteen months after the *Sentinel* article describing Neff's tomato brandy, the following blurb appeared in the paper: "Some of the property belonging to the Neff distillery on Wagner Creek will be sold at Sheriff's sale on the 19th." This sounds somewhat ominous and, taken with the absence of further reports describing Neff's distilling activities, suggests Neff's operation ended about this time.

A fourth Rogue Valley distiller of the period was Raphael Morat. Morat was a Frenchman, born in the foothills of the Pyrenees in 1835. He immigrated to the United States at age twenty-four, spending his first eleven years in California. He settled in the Jacksonville area in 1870, began planting grapes and, within a few years, was producing both wine and grape brandy. The January 29, 1881 edition of the *Sentinel* reported: "Raphael Morat made over 500 gallons of grape brandy at his distillery last year and will make about the same quantity this season. The other distilleries in the county will make about as much more."

Morat had partnered with Alfonzo Chale to open a saloon in Jacksonville and thus had a guaranteed retail outlet for his product. However, in the September 13, 1884 edition appeared this report: "The firm of Morat & Chale, engaged in the saloon business in Jacksonville is hereby dissolved by mutual consent, Raphael Morat retiring. A. Chale will continue the business at the old stand and asks for a continuance of patronage."

So Jackson County's four commercial distillers of 1880 all ceased operation from 1881 to 1884. There was certainly no diminishing of demand, and with the railroad still not having reached the area, there was an obvious opportunity for an enterprising individual—but that's a story for the next chapter.

John Hug, farmer-distiller of Marion County, later became a founding member of the Oregon Pioneer Association. He died in Portland in 1899.

Hug's traveling companion, Peter Britt, having settled in Jacksonville, became the area's resident professional photographer. In the late 1850s, Britt used some of his profits to start Oregon's first commercial winery, Valley View Vineyards. Britt died in 1906.

Frederika Wetterer outlived her second husband and died in 1917. The Wetterer property in Jacksonville was acquired in 1962 by artist Eugene Bennett, who converted the Eagle Saloon building into a gallery and built an

Eagle Saloon in 2014, now part of a private residence. Compare to the photo on page 48. *Photo by the author.*

adjoining residence (the original Wetterer residence having been demolished some years earlier). Bennett died in 2006, and the property is now owned by an ex-California couple.

After selling his saloon and distillery, Joseph Hockett moved to Salem, where his wife, Sarah, died in 1896. He remarried in 1899, and he and new wife Jennie moved to Heppner, a small town in central Oregon, where he became a building contractor. Heppner was wiped out by a flash flood in 1903, which killed about one-third of the town's population, including Hockett and his two young children. Jennie survived, being the only member of the family who knew how to swim.

Thomas Neff, the contrite Confederate, had moved in the 1880s to Central Point, located a little north of Medford. Things apparently did not go well for him, as he spent the last years of his life at the Jackson County Poor Farm, where he died in 1917.

Raphael Morat enjoyed fourteen years of retirement, no doubt continuing to make wine and brandy for his own use, and died in 1898.

DISTILLED IN OREGON

Extra Strong Cider

1 ounce Clear Creek apple brandy (the two-year-old)
8 ounces Oregon hard cider (one of the sweeter varieties)

Pour brandy and cider over ice into a tall glass. Stir gently.

4

A TALE OF TWO DISTILLERIES

In August 1882, two gentlemen arrived in Jacksonville: Nathan Lytle and Nathan Wood. Both were from Union County, Ohio, where Lytle worked as a distiller and Wood owned a saloon (Lytle probably worked at Alfred Watt's distillery in Morrow, the only one in the area). The two were planning a partnership in a distillery operation and, according to the *Jacksonville Sentinel*, were "favorably impressed" with a location north of town. The *Sentinel* went on to say, "Should proper inducements be offered they will remain here. We hope they will come to that conclusion as an enterprise of this kind would create a market for a good portion of our surplus grain."[28]

Wood left for Portland, to determine if there would be any market there for whiskey made in faraway Jacksonville. He probably learned the cost of hauling it over Grant's Pass by wagon would make it uncompetitive with established brands of bourbon and rye brought in by ship. I suspect he didn't believe there was enough local demand around Jacksonville to justify the effort because on September 2, the *Sentinel* reported, "Appearances indicate that N. Wood has gone back on his proposition to build a distillery at this place but N.K. Lytle informs us the enterprise will go ahead nevertheless as some of our merchants propose helping it along. We hope to see it proceed."

Lytle spent the next several weeks lining up investors, and on October 14, the **Rogue River Distilling Company** was formed when Lytle entered into a contract with ten investors whose contributions totaled $1,500 (about $33,000 in 2016 dollars). Under the terms of the contract, Lytle would erect a distillery building, twenty by thirty feet and two stories in height, along

Jacksonville, Oregon, 1883. *Courtesy Library of Congress, 75694932.*

with a single-story warehouse, twenty by thirty-six feet. Lytle was to operate the distillery and receive 50 percent of the profits, with the business being overseen by a treasurer elected by the investors.

The largest stake in the company ($500) was made by Michael Hanley. Originally from Ohio, Hanley had done well in the California gold fields, and then migrated to Douglas County, Oregon, where he met and married Martha Burnett. Michael and Martha arrived in Jackson County in 1857 with two-year-old son John. They purchased a large farm near Jacksonville and prospered over the next thirty years, eventually owning over two thousand acres in Jackson County along with a ranch in Klamath County.

Nathan Lytle began work on the distillery and sent for his family. Wife Katherina, daughter May (age fifteen) and sons William and Ralston (twelve and seven, respectively) arrived during the winter of 1882–83.

Commencing in late December 1882, Lytle began running weekly ads in the *Sentinel* for "good grain of every description."

In February, the IRS appointed W.M. Turner to be the gauger and bonded storekeeper for the distillery.

The distillery was still a work in progress when in early March one of the original investors, George Spooner, sold his interest to John Bailey. Bailey, recently arrived from Virginia, described himself as a "practical distiller" and was evidently intent on hands-on involvement with the operation. In reporting this, the ever upbeat *Sentinel* stated that Bailey "together with Mr. Lytle will no doubt turn out a good quality of liquor and make the business a success."[29] Interestingly, of the two hundred odd "John Bailey" residents of Virginia recorded in the 1880 census, not one listed his occupation as distiller, suggesting Bailey's "practical experience," such as it was, was acquired under the light of the moon.

Production began during the last week of March 1883 and was about one hundred gallons per day, enough to fill two standard-sized (forty-eight-gallon) barrels.

I suspect Lytle had creative differences with John Bailey, his unsolicited distilling partner, because on July 10, he signed a contract with two new partners and paid off the existing ones. Bailey soon left on a stagecoach bound for California; it was probably not a tearful farewell for Nathan Lytle.

The two new partners were John Hanley (Michael's son) and John Hanley's brother-in-law, George Love. Under the terms of the new contract Lytle retained 50 percent ownership of the company, with Hanley and Love each owning 25 percent. In addition to a proportionate share of the profits, Lytle received fifty dollars per month, and Hanley and Love received the spent mash[30] to use as cattle feed.

This contract remained in force until January 7, 1885, when a new contract divided ownership equally among the three partners.

So what sort of whiskey was being produced by Rogue River Distilling? We can't be sure what grains were being used prior to July 1, 1883, but beginning in fiscal year 1884, IRS annual reports provide information on the types of grain being used by American distilleries; the tables presenting the data give only the state totals, but because Rogue River was the only whiskey distillery in Oregon during most of the 1880s, the state's total can be safely attributed to that distillery.

Fiscal Year	Malted Barley	Wheat	Barley	Rye	Corn
1884	421	2,754	31	76	0
1885	484	1,295	72	1,037	199
1886	279	124	135	1,073	0
1887	314	778	0	317	558
1888	0	0	0	0	0
1889	108	2,263	0	29	404

It should be no surprise that wheat was the majority grain for nearly every year, it being the grain traditionally used in Oregon whiskey.

The table's data for 1889 includes usage by a second whiskey distillery in the state, one using less than five bushels per day. Even if this unknown distillery (probably operated by Hezekiah Key in Umatilla County) operated every day (highly unlikely), it could have consumed only 1,825 bushels of the 2,768 bushels used in 1889, and in all probability, it accounted for a much smaller percentage than that used by Rogue.

These figures represent the input side of the equation but offer no clue to the output side. For that, we once again turn to the *Jacksonville Sentinel*, which reported in its September 15, 1883 issue: "The Rogue River Distilling Co. having met with such unbounded success in manufacturing a pure article of Bourbon, Rye and, Corn Whisky, are now preparing to make a run of 20,000 gallons and expect to extend their trade from Frisco to British Columbia by the next season."

Those familiar with modern federally mandated "standards of identity" know bourbon must be 51 percent corn, rye whiskey must be 51 percent rye and corn whiskey must be 80 percent corn and are probably wondering how a distillery that is purchasing more wheat than anything else could be producing these whiskeys, none of which should have more than 49 percent wheat in them (actually less because all of them would need to include at least 6 to 8 percent barley malt). Could it be that what they were doing was putting a small amount of corn and/or rye into the wheat whiskey and calling it something else?

Of course that's what they were doing. By the standards of the day, there was nothing wrong with this, for two reasons. First, federal "standards of identity" did not exist until the mid-twentieth century, so Lytle and his partners were breaking no laws. Second, it was apparently acceptable to assign a name to a whiskey on the basis of a minority grain, the best-known example of this being Canadian whiskey.

For over a century, Canadian whiskey has been colloquially called "rye whiskey," even if rye is only a minority percentage of the grain in a particular whiskey. According to Canadian whiskey reviewer and historian Davin de Kergommeaux, until the late nineteenth century, nearly all Canadian whiskey was made with wheat and a small amount of malted barley. Consumers found these rather bland, so Canadian distillers began to add some rye to the blend. To differentiate this from the previous product, the distillers referred to it as "rye whiskey" despite it still containing a majority proportion of wheat.[31]

I'm sure this is what Rogue River Distilling Company was doing; their "rye whiskey" was mostly wheat with a little rye in it, their "corn whiskey" was mostly wheat with a little corn in it and their "bourbon" was mostly wheat with a little corn and rye in it.

A final consideration in the distillery's favor is the differing yields of whiskey obtained from various grains; although corn, rye and barley reliably produce over four gallons of one-hundred-proof whiskey per bushel, wheat produces only about three. So if a particular batch of mash was half wheat and half barley malt and corn, the wheat's contribution to the final product would be only 40 to 45 percent.

Attentive readers will recall the second portion of the September 1883 quote from the *Sentinel*; by the "next season" (the spring of 1884), Rogue River Distilling expected to be shipping to British Columbia and San Francisco. The company was, in fact, anticipating the arrival of the railroad.

By 1880, the economy had largely recovered from the crash of 1872, and the rail lines were again pushing forward. By 1883, the Oregon & California Railroad had crested Grant's Pass, and surveyors arrived in the Rogue Valley to plot the route of the railroad through the area.

To the dismay of many, the route selected ran well east of Jacksonville, with a depot planned near the railroad crossing over Bear Creek. Land was acquired around this area, and a town was platted out, the name of which was to be Medford.

Once the railroad came through, Medford grew at a rapid pace. In the February 2, 1885 edition of the *Morning Oregonian*, there appeared the following:

> *A LIVELY TOWN.—Medford, Or., in Rogue River Valley, a town only fifteen months old, boasts of 126 houses. They are also building a two-story brick hotel and a block of brick business houses 100 feet front* [sic]. *Corner lots are bringing $600, and fairly located lots, 25x100 feet, for dwellings, $75 to $150 each. A paper will be started this week, and **it is reported that the Jacksonville distillery soon will be moved there**, likewise the foundry from Roseburg* [Emphasis added by author.]

This was surprising news to many local residents, including at least one of the distillery owners (probably John Hanley), who contacted the *Jacksonville Democratic Times* to set the record straight. The following appeared in the paper's February 6 edition:

A GRIEVOUS ERROR. Some poorly informed correspondent has been writing to the Oregonian from this valley and commits a number of blunders. Chief among them is that [of] announcing the removal of the Rogue River Distilling Co.'s works to Medford. This company has no intention whatever of leaving Jacksonville; but, on the contrary, is making a number of substantial improvements here. Such prevarication is hardly edifying.

One must wonder about the "poorly informed" correspondent's source of information, and it's my belief it was Nathan Lytle, who correctly perceived Medford as being destined to become the valley's commercial center. If the distillery had any chance at long-term survival, it would need to move there. Subsequent events support this hypothesis.

The October 17, 1885 edition of the *Sentinel* ran the following article:

NEW ARRANGEMENT. The Rogue River distillery is now owned by John A. Hanley alone, he having purchased the interests of George Love and N.K. Lytle. Caton and Garrett of this place and Ashland have been appointed sole agents for the sale of this liquor and they ask for a share of the trade promising satisfaction in every case.

John Hanley continued with the company for several more years. The distillery produced over fifteen thousand gallons of whiskey in 1886 and by April 1887 had over twenty-two thousand gallons in bonded storage.

It's doubtful Hanley was doing the distilling himself; he had far too many other enterprises to manage. I've found no information that identifies his distiller, but whoever he was, he apparently knew what he was doing, with "the Famous Rogue River whiskeys" being "disposed of in different parts of the state." This is all the more remarkable because in 1883, Portland was reached by the Northern Pacific Railroad, a transcontinental line allowing those bringing in eastern whiskey to transport it by rail as well as by ship.

Meanwhile, Nathan Lytle was trying to start a new distillery in Medford. The September 17, 1886 edition of the *Ashland Tidings* reported Lytle "intends to start another distillery soon near Medford, and prominent citizens of that place are said to be interested in the project."

With so much whiskey in storage, Rogue River Distilling did no distilling in fiscal year 1888 (hence the "0" entries in the table on page 61) but did sell some 8,079 gallons during that year.

John Hanley. *Courtesy Southern Oregon Historical Society.*

Fiscal year 1889 saw the last distilling run at Rogue River Distilling Company, which probably occurred in early 1890. The distillery was deregistered prior to July 1, 1890. I suspect there were a number of reasons for the shutdown, one being that John Hanley's father, Michael, died in 1889 and John found himself with a whole new set of responsibilities.

Another reason was probably the economics of running a distillery in Jacksonville. Although a spur line had been run to the city, this was no substitute for being on the main rail line, as was the case in Medford. There was no distillery in Medford yet, but that was about to change.

⊶⊷

Nathan Lytle's 1886 effort to find investors for a Medford distillery was not successful. I suspect the *Tiding*'s statement "prominent citizens of that place are said to be interested in the project" was probably true, but said citizens were apparently unable or unwilling to venture the necessary capital. Anyone wishing to build a distillery there would need to supply most of the capital to build one as well as the expertise to operate it.

Capital and expertise arrived in the early summer of 1890 in the persons of Frederick Medynski and B. Paul Theiss.

Medynski was originally English, born in London in 1851 to a Polish father and an English mother. After receiving a degree in civil engineering, he immigrated to the United States in 1871, taking residence in Chicago. After working as a marine engineer for several years, he went to work for Chicago's Phoenix Distillery. In the mid-1880s, he was hired by George Kidd, who eventually made him superintendent of Kidd's International Distillery in Des Moines, Iowa. In 1887, Kidd was forced to close the Iowa distillery because of a new local prohibition law, and in 1889, he sent Medynski to La Salle, Illinois, to oversee the construction of a new distillery (much of the equipment, including the still, was designed by Medynski). But before the new distillery began production, Kidd sold it to the Distillers and Cattle Feeders Trust (aka the "Whiskey Trust"), the notorious Peoria-based company seeking to create a whiskey monopoly by buying smaller distilleries and then shutting them down. Medynski was out of a job, and a perfectly good distillery building was sitting idle.[32]

It was also sitting empty because the equipment from the Iowa distillery had not yet been transferred. George Kidd still owned it,[33] and Fred Medynski realized he could leverage his relationship with Kidd to purchase it. All he needed was a partner with money to invest and a location as far away as possible from the Illinois whiskey syndicate.

While in La Salle, Medynski had met Paul Theiss (born in Illinois in 1860 to German immigrant parents). Theiss had worked in a distillery for eighteen months during his late teens, but most of his career was as a clerk and accountant. It was his business management expertise he brought to the enterprise, along with $10,000 to invest in it ($10,000 is equivalent to over $260,000 in 2016 dollars, which suggests Theiss's business management acumen—and probably investing acumen as well—was considerable; he was, after all, only twenty-nine years old).[34]

The prospective partners traveled to the West Coast and, after visiting several locations, decided on Medford. On July 18, 1890, they signed a formal partnership agreement creating the **Medford Distilling and Refining Company**.

Local support for the enterprise was strong, as described in the November 14, 1890 edition of the *Ashland Tidings*:

> *The citizens of Medford are much elated over the prospect of the establishment here of a large business enterprise—something on a larger scale than anything yet attempted in Southern Oregon. It is nothing less than the large distillery and packing house which is to be moved from Iowa to the Pacific coast, and concerning which the Tidings reported a few weeks ago that the representative was looking through Washington,*

Oregon and California with a view to choosing the best location possible. It is a triumph for this valley that it has been selected after so wide a territory has been examined.

The partners were able to secure $5,000 of additional capital from the community, along with a land donation of twenty-two acres at the north end of Medford, and a promised donation of five thousand bushels of corn once the distillery began operation. Additionally, the railroad agreed to run a spur to the distillery property at no charge.

The equipment for the new distillery began its journey west in early December. Also traveling west were the partners' families, which in the case of both men consisted of a wife and a daughter, these being Ella and Henrietta Medynski and Minnie and Geraldine Theiss.

Mid-January 1891 saw the completion of the railway spur to the distillery site, and construction began in earnest. The distillery building itself was 40 feet wide by 160 feet long and stood 60 feet high. It was equipped with all the items originally meant for the stillborn Illinois distillery, including a 150-horsepower steam engine and the large-capacity still designed by Medynski. The distillery building could also store over thirty thousand bushels of grain and could potentially process as many as five hundred bushels per day.[35]

An adjacent building could store over six hundred barrels of whiskey (equivalent to about thirty-two thousand gallons).

Much of the acreage on the property was used for pens to hold cattle and hogs because the distilling operation was combined with a pork- and beef-packing plant. This was a common practice at the time, with the spent grain mash being used to fatten the animals prior to their being butchered.

Such was the scale of operations planned for the facility that it offered full-time employment for at least fifty and seasonal employment for another twenty-five or so. The project had support from most of the community, and the local papers ran frequent and enthusiastic reports describing its progress.

Support was not universal, however. Although there was no mention of it in the papers, there was certainly opposition from temperance activists. This can be inferred from statements made by Medynski and Theiss during the construction phase of the distillery, wherein they claimed most of the output would be medicinal spirits, along with neutral spirits meant for use in colognes and jewelry production. In fact this was never the case, and these statements were undoubtedly meant to deflect criticism from the anti-alcohol contingent—at least until the distillery was up and running.

Whiskey was the intended product, which should have been clear from statements like this one from the January 30, 1891 *Democratic Times*: "Messrs. Medynski & Theiss advise farmers to pay attention to planting yellow corn, rye and barley in large acreage the coming spring, as the distillery intends paying higher than Chicago prices for all these cereals. Yellow corn is preferable to white for distilling purposes, and a ready market will be provided for all that can be raised."

Work on the distillery proceeded over the spring and summer of 1891, with the main building being painted in late July, and a grain elevator being constructed about the same time. The partners hoped to complete construction in time for the autumn harvest.

In September, the IRS appointed J.A. Whiteside to be the resident gauger and Frank Galloway to be the bonded storekeeper. On the eighteenth, the company began soliciting grain sales, offering fifty cents per bushel of corn.

Some six thousand bushels had been acquired by the beginning of November, and the company finally commenced distilling only to discover the amount of water available from its well was insufficient. After the first production run, distilling was suspended until a three-thousand-foot pipe could be laid to connect to the city's water main.[36] This was completed by late December and distilling resumed.

The partners had originally intended to make mostly bourbon, with rye whiskey being a secondary product, but these plans had to be adjusted to reflect the availability of various grains. The *Times* reported on December 4, 1891: "The owners of the distillery find that corn is scarcer than desirable, though they have received an abundance of rye and barley. Our farmers should pay more attention to corn, as it is a profitable crop in every way."

The project experienced another bump in the road in January, when the yeast grower was fired. The individual originally hired had been from a brewery and apparently lacked the expertise to produce yeast that worked effectively on mashbills consisting of mostly corn or rye.[37] Fred Medynski took it on himself to acquire this knowledge and felt sufficiently competent to resume production before the end of March.

In April, the operation rapidly began to take off. A wholesale office was established in July, and Paul Theiss was making numerous trips to points both north and south in order to market the company's products and was, as the *Democratic Times* put it, "selling a great deal of liquor" (yes, "south" means California; the Oregon & California Railroad was completed in 1887). The following January (1893), the paper reported the distillery was running at full capacity, and by January 1894, over forty thousand gallons were in storage.

In March 1893, a local farmer, George Bashford, invested $5,000 and became a one-sixth partner. Although this influx of capital might, at first glance, seem like a good thing, ultimately it would prove to be the undoing of the company.

Determining the exact proportions of grains used by Medford Distilling is not possible. The IRS tables don't help because they aggregate data across all distilleries within a state, and as it happens, in addition to the one in Medford, two small whiskey distilleries and one large one were also producing in 1893 (these being Hezekiah Key's two small distilleries in Weston and Gorham Goodell's large one in Troutdale).

So, for what it's worth, the grain consumption for Oregon whiskey production from 1891 to 1897 is shown in the following table (data from IRS annual reports).

FISCAL YEAR	MALTED BARLEY	WHEAT	BARLEY	RYE	CORN	OATS	MILL FEED
1891	10	0	0	0	120	0	0
1892	2,046	11,277	191	1,648	10,887	20	292
1893	2,214	9,232	0	3,193	3,855	0	483
1894	2,178	19,323	0	2,190	0	0	0
1895	1,346	11,142	0	339	89	0	0
1896	1,701	11,893	0	1,476	1,663	0	197
1897	0	0	0	0	0	0	0

There are a few safe assumptions. Most of the wheat was being used by the other large distillery, this being based on the facts that there are no reports of the Medford distillery using anything other than corn, rye and barley and the other distillery's fate was inextricably tied to the availability and price of wheat (as we will see in the next chapter). It's probably also safe to assume most of the corn used in fiscal year 1892 was used by the other large distillery, based on 1) reports of Medford Distilling's difficulty in obtaining corn, and 2) the other large distillery's having good access to corn during its first year but not subsequent ones (again, this will be explained in the next chapter).

As for how Medford Distilling Company's whiskey reached consumers, an explanation is in order as to how whiskey was distributed and sold during the pre-Prohibition period.

Today, the whiskey produced by a distillery is all bottled before being released for sale; in fact, it's illegal to sell it any other way. In cases where the

Medford Distilling and Refining Co.

DISTILLERS OF

ABSOLUTELY PURE LIQUORS.

Distillery & U. S. Bonded Warehouse at Medford, Or.

Company letterhead. *Re-creation by the author.*

distillery is selling its whiskey to another company planning to brand and sell it as its own product, the whiskey might be shipped in bulk, but it's always bottled before being sold to a distributor, restaurant, bar or store.

In the 1800s, this was the exception rather than the rule. A few companies were bottling all of their whiskey, but this made for an expensive product because until 1903 all bottles were hand made. Instead, most was sent, still in the barrel, to wholesalers, who were known as "rectifiers." The term referred to the alteration of the whiskey by these wholesalers, who rarely bottled or resold whiskey in unaltered form. There were exceptions; distilleries whose whiskey had a good reputation made an effort to find wholesalers they could trust to sell their product unaltered. The **Freiberg & Workum Distillery** in Lynchburg, Ohio, for example, made bourbon sold under the brand name **Cyrus Noble**.[38] This was a popular brand on the West Coast, and the distributor for Oregon and Washington was the **W.J. Van Schuyver Company** in Portland. Van Schuyver would bottle a small proportion of the whiskey, using bottles that had their own name molded onto the bottle itself, with the Cyrus Noble label glued on (other brands sold by Van Schuyver would use the same bottle, but of course had a different label). The bottle, with whiskey in it, was sold to a customer, who later would return and have the bottle refilled by the same retailer, hopefully with the same brand of whiskey. In this sense, bottles of the period were the equivalent of the modern beer growler, being used multiple times.

But most brands were those created by the rectifiers themselves, sold either to retail merchants or to saloons (some larger saloons were also licensed as rectifiers). The more conscientious rectifiers simply blended whiskey from different sources and might combine Oregon-produced whiskey with an inexpensive one from the East, with the brand's label not specifying an origin but simply designating it "Bourbon" or "Rye Whiskey."

Unfortunately, the majority of rectifiers were not conscientious and would "stretch" the whiskey with neutral spirits or water, restoring the color with burnt sugar or concentrated tea and, in the case of watered-down whiskey, restoring the alcohol "burn" with acid or with wood (methyl) alcohol (no, systematically killing off your customers is not a viable long-term business model, but for most rectifiers, greed trumped common sense).

So it's doubtful any of the whiskey shipped by Medford Distilling was sold in straight form; most was probably adulterated by unscrupulous wholesalers.

The one place you could get the company's whiskey in unaltered form was in Medford itself, as Medynski and Theiss opened two saloons, one on the distillery grounds and one elsewhere in Medford, hiring William Taggart to operate the latter one. The saloons were probably opened during the 1893–94 period. To date, I've found no advertisements for the saloons and don't know if they offered anything besides whiskey, but it's hard to believe they didn't offer beer, given the popularity of that beverage. Like most saloons of the era, change was given not in coin but in tokens, which could be redeemed at only the saloon itself, a practice intended to ensure repeat business.

As 1895 opened, things were looking good for the company, but a dispute festering since mid-1893 was about to escalate into open conflict. This centered on the $5,000 investment made by George Bashford. Fred Medynski felt he was entitled to half the amount and could withdraw it as income, while Paul Theiss believed it should be applied toward the company's debt (a little over $10,000 at the time). Neither partner was willing to compromise, and in mid-1895, they chose to dissolve the partnership, after which Medynski sued Theiss. In the subsequent trial a local judge found in favor of Medynski, but Theiss appealed. In early 1900, the Oregon Supreme Court overturned the previous verdict.

In December 1896, the distillery was sold at auction for $2,000. Judge Hilo Hanna decided this was too low, so another auction was held in early 1897. Paul Theiss reacquired the distillery for $3,000, along with 350 barrels of whiskey (for two cents per gallon), with 56 barrels going to other bidders.

Medford Distilling Saloon token. *Photo by the author.*

Theiss never resumed distilling but spent the next several years selling off the over seventeen thousand gallons of whiskey he already had. In 1899, he shut down the saloon at the distillery site and had the other saloon remodeled to additionally accommodate the company offices (saloon manager George Taggart was temporarily laid off during the reconstruction).

In the 1900 census, Theiss's occupation is listed as "wholesale liquors," and it wasn't until later in the year (or possibly in 1901) that the distillery was deregistered. The saloon continued in operation until at least late 1902, and the company still had whiskey to sell in 1904, for in December, a bartender was arrested for serving some of Medford Distilling's whiskey, the hotel where he worked being in the one precinct of the county that had voted "dry" during a November referendum. Also arrested were the two distillery employees who sold the whiskey to the hotel. Charges were dropped against these last two, and the bartender was acquitted at trial in January.[39]

I've found no later references to Medford Distilling & Refining, and I believe by 1905, Paul Theiss had finally disposed of all the whiskey stocks and then proceeded with dissolving the company.

In 1910, the distillery was demolished, and in its article reporting this, the *Medford Mail* offered a possible explanation for why Theiss didn't simply hire a distiller to replace Medynski: "A large business was done for several years, but the inauguration of the fruit industry and the consequent decadence of grain-raising cut off the supply of raw material and the distillery was forced out of business."

In fact a large percentage of the area's farmers had converted to fruit cultivation during this period, and the scarcity of local grain probably was a factor, but I suspect the main reason Theiss didn't resume making whiskey was that his heart just wasn't in it anymore.

⸎

After failing to find investors for a Medford distillery, Nathan Lytle moved his family to Seattle, where the 1892 state census lists his occupation as "collector" but unhelpfully does not specify what it was he collected. He died in 1898 at age fifty-three. Sometime after 1900, his wife and children returned to Ohio.

John Hanley died in 1901 at age forty-six. Wife Mary died in 1904. John's younger sister Alice took over the farm and raised John and Mary's youngest daughter, Claire. Alice Hanley was active in community affairs,

Frederick Medynski and daughter Henrietta in Alaska, 1901. *Courtesy of Southern Oregon Historical Society.*

helping to establish the Oregon Home Extension Service in 1919. In 1924, she ran for a seat in the Oregon legislature, losing to a KKK-sponsored candidate (yes, the KKK; the organization spread beyond the South during the 1920s and was particularly successful in Oregon, with its predominantly white, native-born and Protestant population). After Alice's death in 1940, Claire's elder sisters moved back to Jackson County to live with her. When the last surviving sister, Mary, died in 1986, she left the house and farm to the Southern Oregon Historical Society, which today operates it as a museum.

Frederick Medynski returned to his original occupation, engineering, and patented a number of automotive systems (e.g., braking) during the 1910s and 1920s. He took his daughter Henrietta on a number of trips to locations both near (Crater Lake) and far (Alaska) and served for a while on the Medford City Council. He died in 1933 at age eighty-two; wife Ella died the next year. Henrietta, who never married, operated a millinery shop for many years in Medford. She died in 1970 at age ninety-three and is buried next to her parents.

After closing the Medford Distilling and Refining Company, Paul Theiss became a grocery wholesaler. Wife Minnie died sometime around 1915, shortly before daughter Geraldine left for New York to study music. Upon her return, she became the area's resident concert pianist. She lived with her father until his death in 1940 at age eighty and, according to a number of accounts, never fully recovered from this loss. She died in 1971 at age eighty-three and, like Henrietta Medynski, is buried beside her parents in the Medford Cemetery.

Old Fashioned

The classic whiskey cocktail. Works with either bourbon or rye, or even wheat whiskey.

1 ½ ounces whiskey
1 sugar cube
2 dashes Angostura bitters
1 dash water

Place sugar cube in a cocktail glass and saturate with bitters, add a dash of plain water. Muddle until dissolved. Fill glass with ice cubes and add whiskey. Garnish with an orange slice and a cocktail cherry.

FIRE, FLOOD AND FAMINE

Gorham Blake Goodell was born in Brattleboro, Vermont, on March 13, 1848. He was the eldest son of David and Maveretta Goodell, whose families had been New England farmers for many generations (David and Maveretta were originally from Massachusetts). Gorham was an adventurous youth and decided the life of a New England farmer was not for him. Sometime in his mid-teens he joined the army, accomplished no doubt by lying about his age. He turned seventeen in March 1865, four weeks before Lee's surrender at Appomattox Court House. Three weeks after the surrender, he was promoted to first lieutenant and subsequently discharged.[40]

After the war, he returned to Brattleboro but in 1871 migrated west, ending up in Laramie County, Wyoming, where he became a rancher. In 1872, he partnered with fellow ranchers William and Thomas Sturgis to form Sturgis, Goodell & Co. (which later became the Union Cattle Company).

Goodell probably returned to visit Brattleboro on several occasions, and it was there he married Love Adelaide Frost in 1877,[41] after which he brought both her and his mother back to Cheyenne (his father, David Goodell, had died in 1875).

His cattle business was a successful one, but by 1891, he was ready for a change and moved his family to Portland, Oregon (probably to the great relief of his wife and mother). He was planning to build a combined distillery and feedlot and purchased property in nearby Troutdale for this purpose.

He also wanted a junior partner to manage the operation and enlisted thirty-year-old James Walker for this role. Walker was a Californian, and although his history prior to his hire by Goodell has eluded successful investigation, presumably he had experience in management and/or distillery operations.

The company founded by Goodell was registered as the **Portland Distilling and Cattle Feeding Company**, and construction of the distillery commenced in the summer of 1891 and was completed in late autumn. It was the largest distillery yet built in Oregon, with a daily processing capacity of over one thousand bushels. Its product was probably a wheat/corn "bourbon" using corn and barley malt from the Willamette Valley and wheat from the Willamette and/or Columbia Valley. By early April 1892 quite a bit of whiskey had been produced, with slightly over twenty-nine thousand gallons in storage in the distillery's warehouse.[42] It's probable none of it ever reached market because the oldest was only six or seven months old when disaster struck.

Sometime shortly after 8:30 p.m. on the night of April 7, the distillery caught fire. Newspaper reports the fire was of such magnitude that "the sky was illuminated for miles" and by midnight the entire distillery was nothing but smoking ashes.[43]

Arson was suspected (newspaper accounts state "the building was fired by incendiaries"[44]), but the perpetrators were never identified. The editor of *The Dalles Daily Chronicle* suggested the fire had been started by attendees of the Republican state convention, who "drank up all the whiskey in Portland, and then burned the Troutdale distillery so that the Democrats might be compelled to keep sober during their convention." I'm sure he was kidding. Modern Republicans might do this, but the party was a rather different one in 1892. Most likely the fire was started by prohibition extremists.

Goodell either had good insurance or plenty of capital still available because he immediately began making plans to rebuild. Portland apparently being a hotbed of pyromaniacal prohibitionists, Goodell decided a remote location would be a safer choice and settled on the community of Grants in Sherman County. Grants was located about fifteen miles upriver from The Dalles (between present-day Biggs Junction and Rufus) and was situated on the plain below the bluffs. The project received support from the locals, with area farmers agreeing to provide twenty-five thousand bushels of wheat at a discount, and Goodell proceeded with the purchase of fifteen acres at the edge of town.

With its new location, the company needed a new name and was now known as the **Pacific Distilling and Milling Company** (the site was to house a flour mill with a fifty-barrel-per-day capacity). Construction began during midsummer of 1892 and was completed in early 1893. With the autumn harvest, the distillery was operating at full capacity, and again, hundreds of barrels had been filled with whiskey by the following spring.

It's reasonable to assume the product of the new distillery was made almost entirely from wheat, with a small amount of barley malt. IRS figures for 1893 (which combine the grain utilization data with the distillery in Medford) show a marked reduction in corn consumption, and as later events would show, the fate of the Goodell operation was ultimately determined by the price and availability of wheat.

But before we get to that part of the story, there was yet another disaster looming on the immediate horizon.

The winter of 1893–94 saw heavy snows in the Cascades, resulting in extremely deep snowpack. A warmer-than-normal spring triggered a rapid and massive snowmelt, and both the Willamette and Columbia Rivers rose to levels never before seen (at least not by white people). Portland, at the receiving end of both rivers' current, was completely inundated by June 7, after which the Willamette began to subside.

But the Columbia wasn't done yet, and on June 13, its floodwaters surged through Grants, washing away the entire town, including the distillery, which

Downtown Portland during the 1894 flood. *Courtesy City of Portland Archives.*

was lifted off its foundation and swept into the river with twelve terrified employees still in the building. As the building approached Biggs Junction, the local ferry operator, Lucius Clark, took the ferry out and was able to tow the building to shore, rescuing the eleven men still on it, as well as one who had unsuccessfully attempted to swim to shore.[45]

Astonishingly only the still's worm, a fermenting vat and several barrels of whiskey were lost, and Goodell was so grateful he let Clark keep the lumber from the building, which he used to build a new house (presumably on high ground).

One of the lost barrels was spotted by Ira Rowland of The Dalles, who took his boat out into the raging floodwaters to retrieve it. Despite tugging "manfully" away at it, *The Dalles Daily Chronicle* reported, "It proved too unwieldy for him, and he relinquished his efforts in time to save his life." Several weeks later the *Chronicle* reported several barrels had been recovered by local Indians, who were behaving "not very amicably."

Goodell announced his intention to rebuild, but by this time, he lacked the funds to do it. He let it be known he was willing to relocate to any community which offered a $25,000 bonus to the company. There was support for this in The Dalles, and the issue was taken up during the city council meeting of August 15. The outcome was reported in the next day's *Chronicle*:

> *The matter was thoroughly discussed, although all were agreed at the start that $25,000 was a trifle high for the concession. The Dalles is willing to give a bonus, but does not want to buy a distillery and stock it for someone else. This information was conveyed in more diplomatic language to the company.*

Goldendale, Washington, expressed interest, with proponents offering the argument that lumber and wheat could be purchased for prices lower than at Grants or The Dalles.[46] However, the town could offer a subsidy of only $1,000 and that, along with being ten miles from the Columbia and having no rail service, persuaded Goodell to not locate there.

Ultimately, he decided to rebuild at Grants, despite no one residing there anymore (most surviving residents having moved to The Dalles). Already owning the property was probably the deciding factor. Construction of a new distillery at the site began in the autumn of 1894 but proceeded slowly and ceased in May 1895, when the company went into receivership. Goodell found a new investor, Edgar Carroll of San Francisco, who became the majority owner and company president.

Pacific Distilling Company plant, 1896. *Courtesy of the Columbia Gorge Discovery Center and the Wasco County Pioneer Association.*

With the influx of funds construction resumed with a vengeance. The new distillery was to have nearly double the capacity of the previous one (six fermenting vats as opposed to three, and a flouring mill capable of producing eighty barrels per day as opposed to fifty). By January 1896, the facility was ready for production, with seven hundred head of cattle and hogs on hand for fattening with the distilling operation's spent mash.

But early 1896 saw a bad wheat harvest in Australia, followed by a significant rise in the price of the grain. Oregon and Washington farmers who'd been storing wheat with the intention of selling it to Pacific Distilling instead sent it downriver to Portland for export to foreign markets. By spring, the distillery was operating well below capacity and had on hand more livestock than it could feed. By summer, the situation was even worse, and on July 18, *The Dalles Times-Mountaineer* reported:

> *Owing to the scarcity of wheat, the distillery at Grants has shut down, and will probably not resume operations until about Sept. 1, and Government Storekeeper Herbert is getting a vacation for a short time from the confining duties of watching the stills.*

Summer saw bad weather that damaged the wheat crop in Oregon and Washington, and its price rose further. Over the next few years, it never dropped significantly.

The company periodically announced the distillery would reopen, with the last one reported in the June 30, 1900 edition of the *Chronicle*: "It is said that the Grant distillery will commence operation again about the 1st of October."

But I don't think anyone truly believed it. In fact, in the U.S. census conducted the very same month, Gorham Goodell reports his occupation as "mining speculator," and James Walker gives his as "day laborer."

In fact, the distillery never reopened and was demolished in 1904.

Gorham Goodell eventually found work as a buyer for a large slaughterhouse in Portland. He died in 1913 at age sixty-five. His wife, Love, lived until 1948, dying at age ninety-six. They were survived by two sons and a daughter.

James Walker spent much of the first two decades of the twentieth century as a real estate salesman but, by 1920, was operating a farm in Clatsop County with his brother. He died sometime between 1930 and 1940 and would have been in his seventies. He never married.

―⊷∞⊷―

Before closing the chapter, I'll mention one additional Oregon whiskey distiller of the 1890s, Hezekiah Key. Born in North Carolina in 1840, he served in the Confederate army and after the war moved west, eventually settling in Weston, a town in Umatilla County about fifteen miles northeast of Pendleton. In 1880, he received a homestead grant of 160 acres and later purchased another 640 acres.

He began a small whiskey distilling operation in 1889 and started a second one in 1891 with a young partner, George Badgett (also from North Carolina). Three years later, Badgett married Hezekiah's daughter, Mary Elizabeth.

Key and Badgett's whiskey was probably made mostly from wheat and was sold to local saloons. Like the Goodell distillery in Grants, their operation ceased production in 1896. Being a farmer, Key grew his own wheat, but with the inflated price, he probably could make a higher profit by selling it than by turning it into whiskey. He briefly resumed production during 1902–3 but then shut down for good, his two distilleries being deregistered with the IRS in 1904.

Hezekiah Key died in 1919; his farm still belongs to the Key family and is a designated Oregon Century Farm. Mary Elizabeth Badgett died in 1925, after which George moved to Idaho. He never remarried and died in 1963.

Fire and Flood

Yes, it's a Boilermaker, but with a wheat theme. Drinking this on an empty stomach makes it a Fire, Flood and Famine, but I don't recommend doing that.

1 ½ ounces Ottis Webber Oregon Wheat Whiskey
12 ounces Full Sail Session Wheat

Pour whiskey into shot glass. Pour beer into beer glass. Knock back whiskey. Sip beer at leisure.

6

SUNSET

s described in chapter 2, the Oregon Temperance Society was founded in 1836 by Jason Lee and others whose primary goal was to keep liquor away from the indigenous natives. As we've seen, in 1844, the group and its supporters persuaded the provisional legislature to pass a law prohibiting the manufacture or sale of "ardent" (distilled) spirits; this was, in fact, the high-water mark of the Oregon temperance movement's ability to influence legislation during the nineteenth century. It would be another sixty years before it achieved comparable success.

The prohibition law was repealed in 1846, being replaced by a licensing law that was, in turn, amended in 1852 to further reduce the cost and effort of obtaining a liquor license.

Despite these setbacks, the activists persisted. A number of them gathered in Salem in 1853 to found the Territorial Temperance Society, and the following year, the Portland Temperance League was founded. In 1854–55, these organizations lobbied the territorial legislature to pass a law based on one recently enacted in Maine.[47]

Opposition to such a law was widespread and well organized, with Asahel Bush, publisher of Salem's *Statesman Journal*, leading the charge. Bush was a business associate of William Ladd, who, some readers may recall, was reported in chapter 3 as having made a fortune importing liquor into Oregon. "Maine law" candidates were invariably vilified by the *Statesman Journal* and few were elected, and the lobbying efforts of the temperance groups continued to fail.

This lack of success, combined with the failure of many members to reliably pay their dues, resulted in a succession of organizations being at the forefront of the movement. The Territorial Society was replaced by the Sons of Temperance, who in turn gave way to the Independent Order of Good Templars (IOGT) in the mid-1860s. In 1865, there were sixteen IOGT chapters in the state, with the largest, in Portland, having about 150 members.[48] Considering the state had a population of about seventy thousand, this is not an impressive number.

In the 1870s, the movement began to gain impetus, both nationally and in Oregon. The state chapters of the IOGT gained over five hundred new members in 1874, bringing overall membership to over four thousand.[49]

Along with growth, the movement was evolving in other ways. In its early days, most members advocated temperance, accepting moderate use of alcohol and calling for prohibition of only distilled spirits, but over time, most of them began arguing in favor of the total prohibition of all alcoholic beverages.

The other significant change was an increasing number of women in the movement. By the late 1800s, most American women did not drink alcoholic beverages; improvements in purification technology made metropolitan water safer to drink, as did heating it to brew tea and coffee (these being the beverages of choice whenever women gathered in social settings).

The men in their lives, on the other hand, not only drank but drank a lot. Men of the era spent a large percentage of their time and income in saloons, and their families suffered as a consequence.

In late 1873, the Woman's Christian Temperance Union (WCTU) was founded in Ohio, and other state chapters soon followed. Oregon did not have a chapter until 1880, but in the interim, the state's women were able to follow the organization's activities thanks to Abigail Scott Duniway. Duniway, for many years the state's leading advocate of both prohibition and voting rights for women, published the female-oriented weekly newspaper the *New Northwest*. Duniway's brother, Harvey Scott, was the editor of the *Oregonian* and was ardently opposed to women's suffrage (which had to make for interesting family get-togethers).

The temperance ladies of Portland began organizing, creating groups within their churches (and enlisting their pastors in the crusade), and forming a loose alliance between the groups, with the Methodist church on Taylor Street serving as unofficial headquarters. The initial activities of the "Women's Temperance Prayer League" were described by the *Oregonian* in its March 19, 1874 issue:

Committees have been appointed, consisting of lady members from each of the churches, whose duties are to wait upon the citizens, solicit pecuniary aid with which to carry on the crusade, and also to obtain signers to the temperance pledge. The city has been divided into districts, and certain ladies designated to traverse each district and call on the citizens. Yesterday, in conformity to these arrangements, ladies were circulating freely about with pencil in hand and the pledge, asking for signatures. Their efforts, we learn, were crowned with a very encouraging measure of success, and many persons signed the pledge of total abstinence. Today and tomorrow these labors are to be renewed, until the whole city has been gone over and thoroughly canvassed.

The *Oregonian* reported on March 23 that over two thousand signatures had been collected over the previous four days.

Via Duniway's newspaper, the groups soon learned of the antisaloon crusades being conducted by the WCTU. This activity involved a number of women visiting a saloon, where they would pray, sing hymns and call on the patrons to cease their sinful ways.

On March 23 or 24 (accounts vary), pairs of women arrived at a half-dozen Portland saloons, where they sang hymns and knelt in prayer. In its coverage of these visits, the *Oregonian* reported, "At the conclusion of each hymn and prayer clapping of hands and stamping of feet followed, while on the outside some boisterous individuals would jeer and laugh." The novelty of the situation in fact attracted additional patrons to the saloons, which was, of course, hardly the women's intent.

So at the end of the first day of their crusade, the women were feeling rather discouraged. Hoping to find strength in greater numbers, they resolved to go out the next day as a single group. They visited two saloons the next day, with the only discernable result again being to attract additional patrons to the establishments. So, at least at first, the crusaders were not entirely unwelcome, and at least one proprietor even sent them an invitation to visit his saloon.

But as the novelty wore off, the crowds diminished, and the women began to be considered a nuisance. The size of their group increased, and the effect of their visits was rather intimidating, with many bartenders refusing to serve drinks while the women were present. This happened at the Oro Fino, one of the owners of which was Portland police chief James Lappeus, who, as one might expect, was not a fan of the temperance crusade.

The crusaders had a few victories; as related at the end of chapter 2, that old purveyor of Blue Ruin, Edouard Chambreau, was persuaded to sell his half interest in his saloon and give up alcohol entirely.

The ladies were, however, making more enemies than friends. Probably their greatest antagonist was Walter Moffett, owner of the Webfoot saloon. Over the course of several visits from the women, Moffett became increasingly hostile, shouting obscenities at the women and calling them "damned whores." By April 7, he'd reached the breaking point and called on the police to arrest the crusaders. Chief Lappeus was happy to oblige.[50]

The women invoked constitutional guarantees of freedom of speech and worship, and Judge Owen Denny quickly dismissed the charges.

The crusaders targeted the Webfoot over the next week, and the situation became increasingly acrimonious. A number of husbands and sons began to accompany the women, and on April 16, a full-scale riot broke out that ended when police arrived and rescued Moffett and his employees, who were making a last stand behind the bar.

When the ladies showed up again the following day, Moffett stomped off to the nearest police station and filed disorderly conduct charges against them. Twenty one women were arrested and six held for trial. All were convicted, but the judge was again lenient, with the sentence being only a few hours in jail.[51]

After the trial, the temperance activists focused on the upcoming municipal elections, sponsoring a slate of pro-temperance candidates. These looked to be strong contenders, but a few days before the July election, an anonymous and extremely inflammatory document was circulated. The "Voters' Book of Remembrance" described the patrons of the city's saloons as "whiskey topers [someone who drinks to excess], beer guzzlers, wine bibbers, rum suckers, hoodlums, loafers and ungodly men" and was so offensive that the backlash it triggered led to the defeat of all the temperance candidates.[52]

Nevertheless the temperance activists, both male and female, persisted with their efforts. An Oregon chapter of the WCTU was formed in 1880, with Elizabeth White being its first president. By 1891, the state had eighty-three chapters.

The various temperance groups formed the Oregon State Temperance Alliance, which held annual conventions in Salem from 1871 to 1889. Their efforts finally culminated in a prohibition amendment being placed on the ballot in 1887. The measure was defeated, with 19,172 voting against it versus 7,985 voting for it. The defeat was a primary factor in the dissolution of the alliance two years later.[53]

The WCTU continued to operate at the grass-roots level, being particularly active in churches and Sunday schools, and over time, steadily gained converts.

A new organization, the Anti-Saloon League (ASL), was founded in Ohio in 1893. It went national in 1895 and had a primarily political focus. The ASL promoted the local option, lobbying at the state level for referendums that would allow local governments (county and municipal) to go dry. The argument was "you're not voting for prohibition, you're voting for democracy. You believe in democracy, right?" This seemed reasonable to those who hadn't really thought it through, and the ASL was able to get local-option laws passed in numerous states.

An Oregon chapter was founded in 1903 and in 1904 succeeded in getting a local-option measure placed on the ballot. In the June election, the measure passed, 43,316 to 40,198.[54] In the subsequent November election, six counties—Benton, Coos, Curry, Gilliam, Sherman and Yamhill—voted to go "dry" and several more counties allowed individual precincts to impose local prohibition (Jackson County was one, which led to the court case described in chapter 4).[55]

Most of these elections were close, and those arrested for violating the prohibition ordinances could usually count on there being several sympathizers on their jury. In one celebrated trial taking place in Union County in 1910 (the county had gone dry in 1908), during deliberation the jurors drank the contraband liquor and then acquitted the defendant for lack of evidence (no, really, you can't make this stuff up).[56]

Nonetheless the prohibition movement was steadily gaining members, and it was just a matter of time before they constituted a majority in Oregon.

So what was the effect of growing anti-alcohol sentiment on liquor production in the state? We saw in chapters 4 and 5 the whiskey distilleries of the 1890s closed for reasons unrelated to the prohibition movement, but it may well be that the reason no new ones were started after 1900 was opposition from prohibitionists.

In fact, there are a number of newspaper accounts from 1900 to 1914 reporting individuals who were looking into starting a whiskey distillery, but in no case did anything ever come of it. The explanations for these failures to launch are, for some reason, never reported, and opposition from prohibitionists seems the likeliest cause.

There were still a number of brandy distillers operating, however, and examining production figures for these might provide a better indicator of the effect of public sentiment on production. The table on page 88 presents this data.

DISTILLED IN OREGON

Fiscal Year	Distilleries	Apple	Peach	Grape	Pear	Prunes	Cherry	Total
1899	17	2,029	26	221	36	1,719	0	**4,028**
1900	8	232	50	42	0	95	0	**419**
1901	13	2,358	0	126	50	902	0	**3,436**
1902	12	1,082	174	74	64	1,310	0	**2,704**
1903	6	142	0	65	20	312	0	**539**
1904	5	107	150	121	47	296	0	**721**
1905	5	117	17	0	0	422	15	**571**
1906	2	42	0	0	0	244	0	**286**
1907	2	84	0	0	0	407	0	**491**
1908	2	157	0	0	0	249	0	**406**
1909	2	n/a	n/a	n/a	n/a	n/a	n/a	**1,066**
1910	2	n/a	n/a	n/a	n/a	n/a	n/a	**407**
1911	2	n/a	n/a	n/a	n/a	n/a	n/a	**932**
1912	4	n/a	n/a	n/a	n/a	n/a	n/a	**1,357**
1913	2	n/a	n/a	n/a	n/a	n/a	n/a	**259**
1914	1	n/a	n/a	n/a	n/a	n/a	n/a	**153**
1915	0	0	0	0	0	0	0	**0**

Two comments about the table: first, "prunes" refers to the fresh (undried) fruit, today incorrectly called "plums." Second, the total amount of brandy produced in the peak year of 1899 (4,028 gallons) is not really very much; in that same year, California produced 2,776,669 gallons of grape brandy.

As for the production data presented in the table, there's no obvious decline until 1903–6; up until then, we can assume that low-production years were probably those with poor harvests.

This brings up a point fundamental to understanding fruit brandy production in Oregon; historically, its production has been a function of supply, not demand. Good harvests made for more fresh fruit than the market could absorb, and brandy production was a way of dealing with the surplus (a pattern that continued even after Prohibition, with surplus fruit being the impetus for the creation of Hood River Distillers in the 1930s and Clear Creek in the 1980s).

Most distillers during this period were probably farmers. Lacking IRS tax rolls from the 1890s and 1900s, we can identify only a few, by way of advertisements posted in local newspapers. For example, in the May 2, 1899 edition of the *Salem Capital Journal*, we see August Aufranc advertising "Pure

Home-Made Brandy" made from apples, pears and prunes for $2.50 per gallon. The *Eugene Guard* issue of September 19, 1900, carries a similar ad from I.M. Francis.

Of a handful of commercial fruit distilleries, probably the largest was one located at The Dalles. As described in the previous chapter, the city declined Gorham Goodell's offer to move his whiskey distillery there, but a brandy distillery was another matter, given the frequent fruit surpluses. Thus when A.M. Stringer and an unnamed partner arrived from Virginia in the summer of 1900 and announced their intention to establish a fruit distillery, they received a generally favorable response. The partners located the distillery on the site of the garden associated with the old Methodist mission founded by Jason Lee (a bit of cruel irony, that) and were soon turning apples and prunes into brandy. The *East Oregonian* reported in its November 30, 1900 edition:

> *The distillery, which was established at The Dalles has now been in operation a month and is consuming many hundreds of bushels of apples and prunes which would probably otherwise go to waste, and is creating quite a market for all kinds of fruits which otherwise would not be sold. The distillery has been turning out considerable apple and prune brandy of the finest quality.*

The cold, wet Oregon winter apparently did not agree with Stringer, who announced his retirement in December and departed for the warmer climes of California. His never-identified partner kept the operation going for several more years, but there are no mentions of the distillery after 1905. It probably closed around that time.

In its January 8, 1903 edition, the *Morning Oregonian* ran an article about the community of Myrtle Creek, located in Douglas County about ten miles south of Roseburg. The article contains the following passage:

> *J.S. Dunnavin has a distillery here which has been in operation since 1894 (excepting this year), in making peach, pear, prune and apple brandy. Every gallon made requires a revenue stamp of $1.10 and the capacity of the distillery being about 6500 gallons during the fruit season, the money invested in stamps alone would be $7150, so that Mr. Dunnavin has not been able to run the distillery to its full capacity, which would bring in about $19,000 a year. An addition of about $4000 cash capital is needed. The machinery consists of steam boilers, engine and still, all the cooking being*

done by steam heat. The fruit is here in abundance for operating this plant to its full capacity, and every dollar's worth of brandy manufactured in Oregon adds that much to its worth, by not sending the money out of the state, which is now done.

This sounds like a pretty large-scale operation, but interestingly, James Dunnavin gives his occupation as "farmer" in the 1900 census. It might be he was hoping to transition from farming to full-time distilling, but statewide production figures for this period suggest he never found the capital to do it. His occupation in the 1910 census (when he would have been sixty-seven) is given as "own income," a rather cryptic entry suggesting he might still be distilling, though not openly.

Finally, there are a handful of references to a fruit distillery operation in Medford during the 1909–13 period. A Baptist writer of the time describes this operation as the town's "greatest evil."[57]

Another indicator of increased anti-alcohol sentiment appears in the May 21, 1903 edition of the *Morning Oregonian*, which reported residents in the Holbrook area (about fifteen miles northwest of Portland) had been complaining about an apple brandy distillery in the area. The distillery was licensed to sell its product in quantities of a gallon or more, but those making the complaint claimed it was also being sold by the drink, stating:

The place is frequented by woodchoppers and other laborers, many of whom are frequently intoxicated, and it is charged that the deaths of two men recently drowned not far from the place is to be attributed to drinking too much of this booze. Complaints say that applejack is vile stuff, not fit for any white man to drink.

The *Oregonian*'s editor was apparently not sympathetic to these complaints because the article ends with the suggestion that "it may be that the complainers are prejudiced against a harmless tipple."

With the increasing intolerance toward alcohol production and use, and a number of counties having already imposed local prohibition, it's reasonable to assume illicit production was probably on the rise. Official accounts of the period, however, claim the opposite. The October 8, 1911 edition of the *Morning Oregonian* featured a nearly full-page article entitled "Oregon Moonshiners." Most of the information used in the article came from revenue agents headquartered at the local IRS office, according to whom the peak period for illicit distilling was from 1891 to 1903:

As roads have been built, the districts more thickly settled and revenue agents more skillful and plentiful, the conditions have changed, until now the amount of moonshine whiskey manufactured in Oregon is small, if any at all. The Government agents say there is none—suffice it to say there is none they know about.

I suspect "there is none they know about" is probably the more accurate statement.

Most of the illicit distilling during the period was of fruit brandy rather than whiskey, owing to the high cost of grain (corn, in particular, was not widely planted in Oregon at the time) versus the low cost of fruit. In fact, most harvests yielded a large number of culls, fruit that was judged too cosmetically inferior to send directly to market and was often free for the taking.

In fact, the only producer of moonshine whiskey arrested in Oregon during the first decade of the twentieth century was Columbus Charles "Lum" Davis. Davis, born in 1836 in Indiana, had arrived in Oregon in early 1888. Immediately prior to crossing the Snake River from Idaho, he rescued a young Chinese woman, whose captors were taking her to the mining fields to be used as a sex slave. The woman, named Moye, stayed with Davis, and the two settled in the hills between the Snake River and Baker City, where they raised corn, hogs and two children: James (born in 1889) and Martha (1894).

Davis was first arrested for moonshining in September 1901. Although bail was set at $1,500, he was evidently able to come up with the bond money (a September 12, 1901 article in the *Morning Oregonian* describes him as "quite well-to-do"). His trial was set for November 18, but it's not known if he was acquitted, if he was convicted and only fined or if he simply jumped bail. In any event, he was soon back in the hills making whiskey.

When reports of this reached the IRS, revenue agent John Minto and U.S. marshal Al Roberts were dispatched to find Davis and his still. After a "long hunt in the woods of Eastern Oregon," they located Davis's cabin and distillery, located on a hill near the cabin. Davis was arrested, taken to Portland, tried, convicted and sent to federal prison.[58]

"Lum" Davis might have been the only pre-Prohibition whiskey moonshiner arrested in Oregon, but I doubt he was the only one operating. I also believe that even though a number of illicit brandy producers were arrested, there were many who managed to avoid this fate.

In any case, the incentive for moonshining was soon to be a lot stronger, as the state was moving inexorably toward prohibition. In 1912, Oregon women received the right to vote (61,265 men voting in favor of this versus 57,104 voting against it).[59] Abigail Scott Duniway, now seventy-nine, wrote the proclamation that Governor Oswald West enthusiastically signed into law.

Of the tens of thousands of women who subsequently registered to vote, roughly three quarters were in favor of prohibition.

In addition to women's suffrage, Governor Oswald West was also a strong proponent of prohibition and more than willing to push the limits of the law to further the cause, with the Copperfield affair of 1914 being an infamous case in point.

Copperfield was a small town in Baker County that, according to historian Stewart Holbrook, "had one purpose; namely, to cater to the uninhibited appetites of more than two thousand men who were engaged on two nearby construction projects." The town was dominated by the saloon owners, who included the mayor and the city council members. There were no law enforcement officers, and the overall state of lawlessness resulted in over half the town's population signing an appeal for assistance and sending it to Governor West.[60]

West responded by sending his private secretary Fern Hobbs to restore order, along with state penitentiary warden B.K. Lawson and five members of the state militia. Upon arrival, the formidable Ms. Hobbs[61] immediately imposed martial law, arresting the city officials, shutting down the saloons and confiscating liquor, weapons and gambling equipment. She left Lawson in charge of the town and returned to Salem by way of Baker City, where she convinced the local judge to remove the Copperfield city officials from office.[62]

The saloon owners sued West and Hobbs but lost in every court from Baker City up through the Oregon Supreme Court. The issue was ultimately made moot when a fire of mysterious origin destroyed all of Copperfield's saloons.

In the same year (1914), Governor West and other prohibition advocates succeeded in placing a prohibition amendment on the ballot. The WCTU and the ASL embarked on a campaign to find as many citizens as possible who were not registered to vote and who were inclined toward prohibition. Once located, these individuals were encouraged to register and to sign a pledge to "go to the polls early in the morning and vote Oregon dry." In the three weeks prior to the election, these efforts added 79,000 voters to the

Abigail Scott Duniway signs the proclamation that gives Oregon women the vote. Governor Oswald West is at right. *Public domain.*

rolls.[63] Not surprisingly, the amendment passed, with 136,842 votes in favor and 100,362 opposed.[64]

With the amendment now part of the state constitution, the legislature set about drafting a law to put it into effect. In 1915, it passed the Anderson Act, which prohibited the production, barter or sale of any alcoholic beverage, except by pharmacists who were presented with a doctor's prescription. The act did not ban the possession of alcohol and, in fact, allowed for the personal (not commercial) import of alcoholic beverages. An individual was allowed to bring in two quarts of wine or spirits, or six gallons of beer, and could do this once per month.

The Anderson Act went into effect on January 1, 1916. Oregon was dry— at least, officially.

Abigail Scott Duniway lived just long enough to see Oregon give women the vote and impose prohibition of alcohol; she died on October 11, 1915.

Walter Moffett, the bane of the Women's Temperance Prayer League in 1874, sold the Webfoot in 1875 and booked passage on a ship bound for an island in the South Pacific. He never made it, dying en route. The cause was said to be syphilis, which would explain a lot.

A.M. Stringer, the retiring partner of The Dalles distillery who, for reasons of health, left for California in 1900, does not appear in the 1910 census. Evidently the improved climate was not sufficient to restore his health. The fate of his never-identified partner is unknown.

Moonshiner Columbus "Lum" Davis, who was sixty-seven at the time of his 1903 arrest, was not equal to the severity of prison life, dying at the federal prison at McNeil Island, Washington, on March 3, 1904. Wife Moye and son James continued to live on the farm and were still there for the 1930 census. They don't appear in the 1940 census and presumably died during the 1930s.

Oswald West, possibly the most accomplished governor in state history, chose to serve only one term and returned to private law practice in 1915. He retired in 1945 and died in 1960 at age eighty-seven.

Fern Hobbs likewise resumed practicing law, but joined the Red Cross when the United States entered World War I in 1917. She sailed to France and remained there until 1922. After her return, she served in a variety of positions, both private and public, finally retiring in 1948. She died in 1964 at age eighty.

Temperance Cocktail

I've not tried this, as it sounds awful (but that's what you'd expect from people who don't drink). Try at your own risk.

½ ounce grenadine
1 egg yolk
3 ounces sweet and sour mix

Shake ingredients with ice, strain into cocktail glass.

7

MOONSHINE

Over 100,000 Oregonians had voted against prohibition in 1914, so when the Anderson Act became effective at the beginning of 1916, many took advantage of the provision that allowed the import of alcoholic beverages for personal use. On December 31, 1916, the *Sunday Oregonian* published a table (shown on page 98) showing the number of out-of-state liquor orders placed by Multnomah County residents.

The slight drop in August probably reflects a court decision in July wherein state circuit court judge Robert Morrow declared unconstitutional the limit on imported alcoholic beverages. Basing his ruling on a recent U.S. Supreme Court decision regarding the Webb-Kenyon Act (a 1913 federal law intended to support states wishing to control the import of alcoholic beverages), Judge Morrow held that the lack of a law prohibiting possession of such beverages in Oregon meant a limit on personal imports was not legal.[65]

Legal scholars examining the Supreme Court decision argued that a total ban on importation of alcohol into the state would be legal (a Supreme Court decision in January 1917 upheld this interpretation), so prohibition advocates lost no time getting an amendment for this placed on the November 1916 ballot. It passed with 114,932 votes in favor and 109,671 opposed (another amendment, to legalize the manufacture and sale of beer, was defeated 140,599 to 85,973).[66] The effect on liquor orders is clearly reflected by the November and December figures in the table on page 98 with Multnomah County drinkers trying to get a final delivery before the new law took effect on January 1.

January	784
February	3,317
March	6,600
April	8,683
May	10,377
June	11,867
July	14,089
August	13,284
September	15,245
October	17,332
November	32,416
December (estimate)	36,000

Many Oregonians also took advantage of the Anderson Act's allowance of alcohol for medicinal purposes. Portland druggists filled 334 prescriptions for medicinal alcohol in January 1916; the number filled the following September was 4,740.[67]

With neighboring California being a wet state (at least until the advent of national Prohibition in 1920), it became a convenient source of liquor (Washington was not an option because that state had gone dry at the same time as Oregon). By mid-1917, railway porters had established a lucrative bootlegging operation, bringing a steady supply of liquor from Oakland, California, to Portland via the Oregon & California Railroad.

The year 1917 saw the beginning of George Baker's sixteen-year reign as Portland's mayor. Baker was originally an actor and theater owner but gravitated to politics during the mid-teens. With the advent of state prohibition, he saw an opportunity to get rich and to do it via the rather astonishing scheme of using the city government as a bootlegging organization. Once in office, he recruited Portland police chief Leon Jenkins into the operation and turned to his close friend Bobby Evans to handle the extra-governmental side of things.[68]

Evans was an ex-boxer turned boxing promoter and, in this capacity, came in contact with a lot of young toughs looking for work. By the 1920s, he controlled a large network of smugglers, moonshiners and bootleggers operating in the Portland area, all of whom forwarded to him a percentage of their revenue. Evans, in turn, paid county and city officials to provide immunity for his people and their activities; one estimate of the amount was $100,000 per month ($1.3 million in 2016 dollars).[69] This money was in turn distributed throughout the official infrastructure, from police officers up through (presumably) the mayor.

Much of the imported liquor (Caribbean rum, Canadian and Scotch whiskey, aka "the good stuff") was distributed by the Portland Police Department. Senior government officials and the well-heeled friends of the mayor did not want low-life thugs showing up at their doors, so police officers frequently made such deliveries. Floyd Marsh, head of the vice squad during the mid-1920s, described one such delivery:

> *I was ordered to take some whiskey to a City Commissioner who had a summer house near Mt. Hood. I went to the Police Station and loaded my car with 11 quarts of bonded Scotch Whiskey and headed for Mt. Hood. Since I would be going in the wrong way for an alibi, I kept my eyes peeled for Federal Agents.*
>
> *As I left the station, I passed a Federal Agent who asked, "Where are you going, Marsh?" and I replied, "To set a little bait," (give whiskey to informers). This was just in case he knew I had the whiskey.*[70]

As you might expect, the Portland PD focused most of its enforcement activities on those operating outside the Evans network. Ethnic minorities, in particular, were targeted. As Marsh described it in his memoirs, "The poor working class of the Italian people, unable to pay off the authorities, were the ones arrested and prosecuted."

Arrest was one thing, acquittal quite another. With half of Multnomah County having voted against prohibition, juries usually included members inclined to be lenient, and there were additional instances of jurors drinking the evidence. The *Oregonian* denounced this behavior and its underlying attitude in its March 30, 1918 issue: "The levity which has greeted the indiscretion of the jurors who drank part of the evidence in a bootlegging case is indicative of a sentiment which has a wider prevalence than it should. That sentiment makes enforcement of the law more difficult."

Consequently, when an independent bootlegger or moonshiner was acquitted, the Portland PD would make an extra effort to make another arrest, one that would hopefully achieve a more desirable outcome. Floyd Marsh, in his memoirs, described an operation taken against Floyd McReynolds, who owned a small taxi company and who did a little bootlegging on the side. McReynolds had been acquitted of an earlier charge, so the Portland PD contrived a sting operation intended to obtain another arrest. This involved phoning in three cab request calls in a row, requiring McReynolds to personally respond to the third one. McReynolds didn't know his prospective passenger was actually a police plant and was carrying a gallon of moonshine. Two officers—Roy Cox and John Seeley—were waiting in a nearby car. As recounted by Marsh,

> *When McReynolds pulled out with his passenger (planted by Cox), the two special officers ran him to the curb. At the same time the special passenger jumped out of the cab and ran in between two buildings leaving the gallon of moonshine in the cab. When the two special officers walked up to the cab, McReynolds was surprised to find himself and a gallon of moonshine in the cab alone.*

McReynolds was convicted after this arrest, which eliminated one (small) competitor for the police-protected Bobby Evans organization.

I should mention here that Marsh uses the term *special* to denote members of the city's so-called secret police squad. "So-called" because the existence of the group was reported on several occasions by the *Oregonian*, which means it wasn't really all that secret.

With the Portland PD enforcing the law on a selective basis, only the agents of the Treasury Department's Bureau of Prohibition could be relied on to not play favorites. Even so, there were numerous instances of agents taking bribes or even joining the ranks of the bootleggers; with the agents' annual salaries ranging from $1,680 to $2,000 ($22,861 to $27,215 in 2016 dollars), the temptation had to be hard to resist.[71] A number who did succumb to temptation were caught, and their trials were eagerly followed by the press.

The 1926 trial of former agent Arthur Christensen was noteworthy because one of the prosecution witnesses was Roy Moore, who conducted a moonshining/bootlegging operation for the Evans organization. Moore, variously known as "A.H. Moore," "A. Roy Moore" and "Roy A. Moore," first appeared on the Portland crime scene in 1921 when he and two companions robbed a wagon carrying a circus payroll.[72] Moore and one of the other robbers were caught, tried and convicted. He served two years in prison and upon release came in contact with the Evans organization, which put him in charge of the portable moonshining operation. The still, estimated at around one-thousand-gallon capacity, was just small enough to be transported in Moore's Dodge truck and was carted around the rural areas surrounding Portland. Moore and his crew would operate it in a particular location for no more than three months at a time, after which it was loaded back into the truck and moved again.

The Prohibition Bureau had been following Moore's activities and by July 1926 had "completed what was considered an iron clad case against Roy Moore in which he was charged with some eleven overt acts."[73] Moore and several of his gang were arrested. At the November trial, the gang's attorney argued that because Moore and others had admitted to being bootleggers when testifying for the prosecution in the Christensen case, they were immune from any crimes committed up to that point. The judge agreed, and the charges were dropped, which put the Prohibition Bureau back to square one with respect to bringing Moore to justice.

The bureau was not about to abandon its efforts to prosecute Moore and his cohorts. "The United States Attorney at Portland, Oregon has been and still is very anxious to get a case against Roy Moore" reads a bureau memorandum from 1928, which goes on to state, "It is therefore requested that a case jacket against Roy Moore, subject: 'Conspiracy to violate the National Prohibition Act on the part of Roy Moore, et al,' be forwarded to this office for assignment."[74]

Bureau agents had never stopped investigating Moore, and a case jacket was quickly filled with incriminating evidence. Examination of this evidence provides revealing insight into how many of these moonshiners operated.

During April and May 1926, Moore and company were operating in a barn located on the Hickman farm in Yamhill County. They were using a newly constructed still because the one previously used had mysteriously disappeared. This still had a capacity similar to the previous one and could produce 150 to 160 gallons of moonshine per day, which was sold for four dollars per gallon. [75]

Moore had not had time to set up the still in a new location when he was arrested in July. After the federal judge dismissed the charges in November, Moore and his crew set up the still on a farm owned by I.M. Elliot of Skamania County, Washington, for which they paid farmer Elliot $600 per month. Gang members Frank Brown and Robert Anderson operated the still while Moore, Wesley Lievsey and Robert Specht obtained supplies as well as transported the finished product across the Columbia River for storage at a farm belonging to Robert Fitzgerald. Bottling took place at the Vern Hilyard farm on Boring Road near Gresham, which had a storage capacity of two thousand gallons. Hilyard received $100 per month for the use of his property.[76]

In March 1927, the still was moved to an uninhabited farm in Tillamook County. In April, a middle-aged couple, Clarence and Frances Hannenkratt, were visiting a nearby farm where they were storing a truck. While Clarence was performing some maintenance work on the vehicle, Frances wandered off to pick flowers and came on the distilling operation. The two gang members running the still (probably Brown and Anderson) engaged Frances in conversation outside the building; the three were eventually joined by Clarence, who had come in search of his wife. The Hannenkratts were taken inside, shown the operation and joined the moonshiners for several tipples, after which Clarence was given a pint to take with him.

Upon hearing of this, Moore visited the Hannenkratts and offered them a "present" for their guarantee of silence. The Hannenkratts replied that they did not have to be bought; they tried to attend to their own affairs and not meddle in other people's business. The amicable exchange finally ended with arrangements being made for a social outing, and two weeks later, Moore and wife Elizabeth, the Hannenkratts and several other gang members and their wives all got together for a picnic on a beach near Tillamook (I don't know what they were drinking, but I don't think it was sarsaparilla soda).[77]

Despite the Hannenkratts' promise of silence, Roy Moore decided it was time to move the still again, this time to a location on a farm belonging to Harry Hurst in Clackamas County. Hurst was paid $500 per month. The still was operated until mid-July, when it was moved to another location.[78]

Yamhill County barn that housed Roy Moore's still. *Courtesy of the National Archives, Seattle.*

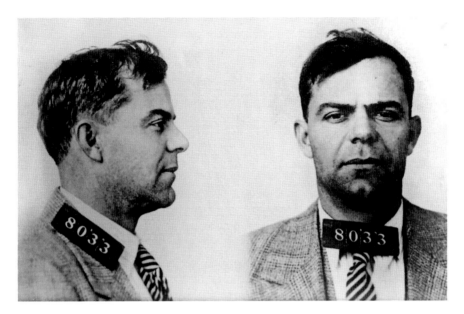

Roy Moore. *Courtesy of the National Archives, Seattle.*

The Prohibition Bureau had been surreptitiously monitoring all this, and every time Moore vacated a premise, it would bring in its owner and present him with the choice of cooperation or facing accessory charges. All were willing to testify for the government; this included the Hannenkratts, who decided sacrificing their principles was preferable to sacrificing their freedom.

The bureau continued to follow Moore's activities and in mid-1928, when seeking indictments for Moore and his associates, presented the evidence associated with the Skamania, Tillamook and Clackamas County operations. Moore and a number of his gang were arrested in September 1928 and tried the following January. Most were convicted; Moore received the most severe sentence (two years prison time and a $1,000 fine), with others receiving shorter terms and lighter fines (wife Elizabeth was fined $1,000 but served no time).[79]

Moore's still was not discovered. At trial, gang member Robert Specht claimed it had been destroyed by the owner of the latest farm to host the operation but did not disclose any information about the farm or farmer.[80] It's been reported the still was in fact taken over by Joseph Brown (another bootlegger associated with Bobby Evans).[81]

Over the course of the two years prior to his arrest, Moore is estimated to have made a net profit of $20,000 ($278,500 in 2016 dollars).[82]

Joe Brown (actual name Nicholas Tingas) ran a larger operation than did Roy Moore, with usually at least six stills in service in and around Portland and a ring of over thirty individuals to run the enterprise. Occasionally, one of the stills was discovered and seized by authorities, but his attorney, Walter Tooze, was exceptionally good at getting these released. In fact, Tooze was so good at getting things done for the Brown ring that when the Prohibition Bureau finally took down the group in 1930 (seizing no less than seven stills; one of 1,000-gallon capacity, four of 500-gallon capacity and two of 120-gallon capacity),[83] the U.S. attorney included Tooze among those charged as conspirators. In the subsequent trial, Brown was convicted; Tooze was not.

The George Baker/Bobby Evans enterprise supplied the Portland area with both imported liquor (for the well-to-do) and moonshine (for everybody else). For the rest of the state, demand was met by local moonshiners, of whom there was a more than sufficient number.

Much of the moonshining activity took place east of the Cascades. Hills, canyons and ravines created numerous locations that offered concealment from federal agents (of which there were only eight to cover the entire 98,381 square miles of the state) and from local law enforcement officers, many of whom were either sympathetic to the moonshiners and/or easily bribed. The area was in fact producing more than it could use, with the surplus being sent west. Wrote area historian David Braly, "At a certain late hour of the night, the sky around Prineville [a town about 30 miles northeast of Bend] would suddenly light up because of hundreds of stills being fired at the same time."[84]

An invaluable insight into the methods, life and perspective of one of these eastern Oregon moonshiners is provided by Ivan Ray Nelson, who published *Memoirs of an Oregon Moonshiner* in 1976. Born in Missouri in 1897, he served in the navy during World War I before he drifted west, ending up in Malheur County, Oregon, in 1922. He found work as a ranch hand but "decided there were easier and more profitable ways" to make a living. He began moonshining in late 1923, first with one partner, with whom he parted company in early 1924, and then with another partner, working in the Lost Creek area near Vale.

In his book, Nelson differentiates his own moonshine recipe from that made in "the mountains of the Southern states," which he claims was made entirely from malted corn (not true; moonshine in the South usually contains a small amount of malt [corn or barley], with the bulk being sugar and cracked corn, and the relative ratio of the last two being at the discretion of the distiller). For his own product Nelson was using, by weight, half rye and half sugar, with the rye being purchased from local farmers. Nelson does not mention adding malt or malt syrup to convert the rye starch to sugar, but he must have done so. Forty pounds of rye and forty pounds of sugar was mixed with twenty gallons of warm water in a fifty-gallon barrel and allowed to ferment. The barrels were secondhand; Nelson steam-cleaned them to remove anything that could contaminate the mash.[85]

Nelson does not give his distillation proof but does state that he cut the moonshine to 120 proof (60 percent ABV) before putting it into small barrels for a few weeks of aging. These were ten-gallon barrels, pre-charred on the inside and purchased new. This size was much smaller than barrels traditionally used to age whiskey (about fifty- to fifty-five-gallon capacity). But the smaller barrels had a higher wood-to-liquid ratio, and the spirit picked up color faster. When ready to sell, Nelson would further cut the "whiskey" to between 105 and 117 proof.

Nelson called his recipe and process "the Oregon method," suggesting that it was the same used across the state. In fact, there was a lot of variability in recipes, and in the Willamette Valley, corn was typically used instead of rye. The ratio of grain to sugar was also usually lower; one Prohibition Bureau case file reports a small-scale moonshiner purchasing four one-hundred-pound sacks of sugar along with one one-hundred-pound sack of cracked corn and, because he was doing this on credit, asking the store clerk to record it as something else. Malt syrup was used more often than dried malt for catalyzing starch into sugar.

One thing that was nearly universal was the use of small barrels for aging. Ten gallons was the most popular size, and moonshine aged in these for a month or so was almost as dark as legitimate whiskey aged several years in a fifty-gallon barrel. If the moonshine had a good percentage of grain in the mash (over 30 percent) it might even taste a little like whiskey. Of course, with this being the only thing available, people couldn't afford to be too picky, so they bought it.

And they bought a lot of it. Oregon newspapers of the Prohibition period were filled with accounts of people drinking moonshine to excess, despite numerous dire warnings about its safety. Perhaps my favorite article is from the April 4, 1922 edition of the *Oregonian*, which reported:

> *Pupils of the school at Alfalfa, 20 miles east of Bend, today broke up the regular sessions of the school by riotous conduct and forced the teacher to summon help to quell the disturbance, when they became drunk on moonshine whisky.*

Five of the students, ranging in ages from 12 to 16 years, came to school with bottles of moonshine, according to reports reaching here, and proceeded to treat their friends, so that in a short time the entire student body became so unmanageable that the instructor was forced to call for help.

No, it's not funny that teenagers were getting drunk at school. What is significant about this story is that it highlights the easy availability of liquor despite Prohibitionists' efforts to completely eliminate it. In fact, legal-but-regulated sales would have probably kept it out of the hands of these children.

By the end of the 1920s, it was increasingly clear that Prohibition was a failure. The advent of the Great Depression created a demand for the jobs destroyed by Prohibition, not just in the manufacture of beer, wine and spirits, but also in ancillary industries such as barrel- and bottle-making.

In Portland, Prohibition had been doomed from the start, considering George Baker had turned the city government into a de facto bootlegging ring. The corruption of the Baker administration was its undoing, however, and by early 1932, enough signatures had been collected to hold a recall election, despite Bobby Evans's efforts to intimidate the mayor's opponents.[86] Baker barely survived the election, but with the loss of his political base and the end of Prohibition on the horizon, he decided against running for reelection the following autumn.

In a special election held in July 1933, of the nine measures on the ballot, those of greatest interest were numbers 1 and 8. The first one concerned the Twenty-First Amendment to the U.S. Constitution, which repealed the Eighteenth Amendment (the Prohibition amendment). This passed, 136,713 to 72,854. Measure 8 was the repeal of Oregon's own prohibition amendment; this passed by an even wider margin, 143,044 to 72,745.[87]

The Twenty-First Amendment was ratified on December 5, 1933. For the nation, for Oregon and for Portland, the long night was finally over.

———

George Baker's retirement was brief; he died in 1941 at age seventy-two. The October 18, 2012 edition of the *Portland Mercury* listed him as the second-worst mayor in Portland's history (the distinction for being the worst belongs to William Farrar, who, after his inauguration in 1862, announced he needed to take three months leave to finish some personal business. He was never again seen in Portland).

Bobby Evans, who had acquired more visibility than he wanted during the campaign to recall Baker, maintained a lower profile from that time on. He continued to remain active in Portland boxing promotion, gambling and racketeering. He died in 1974 at age eighty-one.

Vice squad chief Floyd Marsh left the Portland PD in 1931 to mine gold in Arizona. During a return visit to Portland in 1932, he met Leona "Bo" Calhoun and married her soon after. They had one son, Dennis, born in 1941. Floyd died in Portland in 1979 at age eighty-one; Leona had died in 1976 at age sixty-six.

After release from federal prison in 1930, Roy Moore found he was no longer needed by the Evans organization, so he returned to his first vocations: burglary and armed robbery. His most infamous exploit was in 1945, when he and a partner burglarized a number of businesses in Brownsville, after having dispensed with a third companion who they decided was unnecessary ("dispensed" meaning murdering him and dumping his body in a creek near Camp Adair). He served a number of terms in prison, entering the Oregon State Penitentiary for the final time in 1953, where he died in 1960 at age seventy-one. He was apparently still on good terms with at least one of his two daughters, who paid for a plot and headstone in City View Cemetery in Salem.

Clarence and Frances Hannenkratt, who'd married in 1912 while in their early thirties, never had children and, after testifying against Roy Moore in 1928, lived out quiet lives in Tillamook. Clarence died in 1951 at age seventy-one and Frances in 1956 at age seventy-nine.

Walter Tooze, after being acquitted in 1931, continued to practice law but became more selective about his clients. He became a member of the Oregon Supreme Court in 1950, where he served until his death in 1956 at age sixty-nine.

Ray Nelson shut down his moonshining operation in 1933, after the end of Prohibition. He'd married Etta Sevey in 1928, and they started a ranch near the site of his moonshining operation. He retired to Prairie City, where he died in 1992 at age ninety-five, having outlived Etta, who died in 1986 at age seventy-six.

Etta Nelson Old-Fashioned

If Etta liked to make old-fashioneds with Ray's moonshine, they probably tasted something like this.

DISTILLED IN OREGON

1 sugar cube
2 dashes Angostura bitters
1 dash water
1 ounce Rogue rye whiskey (probably the youngest you can get)
1 ounce overproof (151 proof) white rum

Place sugar cube in cocktail glass and saturate with bitters, add a dash of plain water. Muddle until dissolved. Fill glass with ice cubes and add whiskey and rum. Stir and then garnish with an orange slice and a cocktail cherry

SUNRISE AND ECLIPSE

It being obvious that Prohibition was on the way out, in early 1933 Oregon governor Julius Meier created a committee to study the issue of alcoholic beverage regulation, appointing Portland physician William Knox to lead the committee. The committee recommended the adoption of a system like that of Canada, where all alcoholic beverages were sold in government-owned stores. The legislature ultimately enacted a law that implemented a modification of this, with only distilled spirits and fortified wines being sold in state stores.

The law, known as the "Knox Law" even though it varied quite a bit from the committee's recommendations, required licenses for the manufacture, sale and serving of alcoholic beverages. The law also created a new state agency, the Oregon Liquor Control Commission (OLCC), to provide licensing services, to enforce the law's provisions and to operate the state stores and function as a purchasing and distribution entity for them.[88]

This system, with only a few modifications, remains in effect today. Of course, some changes have been made. Originally, distilled spirits could not be served by the glass; a referendum in 1952 changed this. As for retail sales of distilled spirits, eventually this shifted to private stores; however, the liquor remains the property of the state until sale to the consumer. Store owners are OLCC "agents" and receive commissions from the agency rather than direct profits from sales.

Governor Meier signed the new law on December 15, 1933, ten days after national Prohibition ended. It was another two months before any liquor stores opened; on February 15, four stores in Portland opened their doors. Over the next month, nineteen more opened around the state. Of course, having a place to sell liquor and having liquor to sell are two entirely different things, as the whole production and distribution system had to be rebuilt from the ground up. As a result, illegal channels continued, with Prohibition-era bootleggers such as Joe Brown still operating (Brown was arrested in July 1934 with twenty gallons of "untax-paid" distilled spirits in his possession).[89] High taxes were another reason the illicit traffic continued, particularly in control states like Oregon, where the government hoped to take advantage of its monopoly to generate a lot of revenue.

It was partly to meet the demand for spirits but perhaps even more to address the issue of surplus fruit that three Hood River "orchardists" decided to start a distillery to produce fruit brandy. Every harvest saw a large percentage of the crop culled because the fruit was cosmetically flawed. Turning it into brandy was the traditional method for dealing with this surplus and had been the impetus for the creation of The Dalles distillery thirty-four years before.

Culled apples from 1934 float in a Columbia River slough. *Courtesy of Hood River Distillers.*

The three Hood River orchardists were Albert Peters, Edwin "Ted" Pooley and Edward McClain Jr. None were Oregon natives; in fact, all three were from wealthy eastern families. They'd met while attending Asheville School, an exclusive preparatory school in North Carolina.[90]

Peters and Pooley were the first to arrive in Hood River. The 1910 census shows both living there and giving their occupations as employers in the fruit industry. Why they selected faraway Hood River, Oregon, to be their home is not definitively known. Albert Peters's granddaughter Jill Stanford stated that Peters convinced Pooley and McClain to come to Hood River, so it may be that he had previously visited the area and decided it was where he wanted to live.[91]

Peters, who was born in New York and whose family had moved to Cincinnati before 1900, graduated from the Asheville School in 1906 and from Cornell University in 1910. In 1912, his fiancée from Cincinnati, Marguerite Millikin, came to Oregon, and they were married in the tiny town of Union. A daughter, Betty, was born in 1914, followed by another, Marguerite, in 1917.

Ted Pooley was from Philadelphia, where his father owned a furniture factory. Evidently he was not a great scholar, as there is no record of his actually graduating from the Asheville School. He did spend one year at Harvard (1907–8), majoring in agriculture (yes, Harvard had a School of Agriculture until at least 1936). After coming to Oregon, he met a Portland native, Dorothy Newhall, whom he married in 1911. A son, Edwin Randolph Jr., was born in 1913 and a daughter, Barbara, in 1916. By 1920, he'd established the Pooley Fruit Company and in 1927 built a large house in one of his orchards.

Edward McClain of Ohio, whose family was probably the wealthiest of the three, graduated from the Asheville School in 1907 and went on to Cornell. After graduation, he spent several years traveling around the western United States, purchasing ranch land in Texas and Utah and orchard acreage in Oregon. He married Mildred Wood in Utah during 1917, and she gave birth to a daughter, Edna, in January 1918. The marriage was not successful, and Edward and Mildred divorced in 1919. His attorney for the divorce was located in Portland, and it was while visiting the offices there that he met legal secretary Meredith Sheldon White, whom he married in late 1919 after his divorce was final. During the 1920s, they established residency in Los Angeles, where they had their winter home. The summer home was to have been a large house purchased in 1923 and located on Van Horn Butte near Hood River, but according to Jill Stanford, Meredith McClain did not like

(*Left to right*) Marguerite and Albert Peters, Ted Pooley and an unnamed feathered friend. *Courtesy Elizabeth Dameron, Albert Peters's great-granddaughter.*

HRD wooden fermention tanks, circa 1935. *Courtesy Hood River Distillers.*

living in Hood River, preferring to stay in Portland. The house was vacant most of the time, probably occupied only when McClain was in Hood River on business.

It was probably on one of these visits that McClain got together with Peters and Pooley and one of them proposed a distillery as a solution to the surplus fruit problem. They agreed to move forward with it, and **Hood River Distillers** (HRD) was established in 1934. The partners applied for a license from the IRS and received DSP-OR-1, the first license granted to an Oregon distiller after the end of Prohibition (for some reason the OLCC did not issue a license to HRD until 1950). Property was acquired at the east end of State Street in Hood River, and construction began. Ted Pooley persuaded his seventy-seven-year-old father, Edward, to come out of retirement and move from Philadelphia to become general manager, and Hood River High School chemistry teacher Jesse Crenshaw was hired to serve as the company chemist. Edward McClain was the company president, Albert Peters the vice-president and Ted Pooley the secretary-treasurer.

The distillery was ready in time for the 1934 harvest and began turning out fruit wine as well as apple and pear brandy. For the first couple years, the company was selling its product in bulk to other companies, but in 1936, it introduced its "Old Delicious" brand of fruit wines and brandies. A few years later, the distillery began producing kirsch, a cherry brandy.[92]

Production received a boost in 1935 when a large Lummus continuous still was installed. At thirty-six feet in height, the column for this was so tall it extended two floors above the distillery room, requiring holes to be cut to accommodate it. This still, probably the largest to ever operate in Oregon, could produce 1,500 gallons of brandy per day. HRD was now drawing on ten thousand acres of orchards for supply and consuming over 460,000 boxes of apples per year.

The apple brandy received two years of barrel aging. The pear and cherry brandies were not barrel aged and today would be labelled eau de vie, but I doubt they were labelled as such by HRD. The HRD brandies were not high-end products and sold for ninety cents per pint, relatively inexpensive even in those days. There was a good market for such spirits (particularly the apple brandy), and the company was making a good profit.

On the personal side, life was not going well for Albert Peters or Ted Pooley. In 1934, while Albert was playing golf with Dorothy Pooley, they observed a column of smoke rising on the other side of the valley. Evidently Dorothy had better eyesight than Albert because it was she who realized the smoke was coming from the Peterses' home, Far View. They arrived home to discover the

Column of the Lummus still (*at right*), December 1935. *Courtesy Hood River Distillers.*

house staff had managed to save much of the contents (including a Steinway baby grand piano), but the house itself was beyond saving. Peters decided against rebuilding, and the family moved into a house in Hood River. Then, in January 1935, his wife, Marguerite, died at age forty-six.

As for the Pooleys, 1936 saw the death of their twenty-three-year-old son Edwin. During 1937, both Ted Pooley's brother and mother died. With the death of his wife, Ted's father, Edward, probably decided to retire from his position as HRD general manager; his entry in the 1940 census lists no occupation and no income.

When the United States entered World War II at the end of 1941, HRD was directed to begin distilling high-proof alcohol for industrial purposes and produced this exclusively until the end of the war in late 1945.

The war also claimed the life of the Pooleys' son-in-law, Edmond Labbe. Their daughter, Barbara, married Edmond in 1939; they had one son before Edmond was killed in 1942.

In 1945, Edward McClain's wife, Meredith, died. Like Marguerite Peters, she was only forty-six at the time of her death.

In 1947, the partners decided to sell the distillery. All had recently turned sixty, and I suspect that with the cumulative effects of age and emotional trauma, they had lost all enthusiasm for the business. The new owners were three West Coast families who still own HRD today. One of the new owners was Ezra Royce, and his grandson Ronald Dodge has been the company CEO since 1999.

HRD continued to make fruit brandy into the 1960s, but during the early 1950s, the new owners took note of the rising popularity of vodka and decided to introduce their own. HRD's brand—"Baron Rothschild"—reached store shelves in 1955 and was an immediate success (it's currently sold as "B.R. Rothschild"). The company soon added a second vodka, this one carrying an "HRD" label, and this product is today the bestselling spirit in Oregon (though the one

Label for "Old Delicious" apple brandy from the 1930s. *Courtesy Hood River Distillers.*

generating the most revenue is Jack Daniels, a bottle of which costs three times as much as a bottle of HRD vodka).

The column still at the distillery could produce the 190-proof spirit required to make vodka, but the distillery at Hood River was set up to process fruit. The company soon recognized that fruit-based vodka could not be sold at a competitive price. It would be more cost-effective to purchase grain-based ethanol from Midwest producers and use that to produce its vodka, so HRD switched to this alternative.

In the 1960s, HRD added a full selection of liquors (gin, vodka, tequila, bourbon, et cetera) when it acquired the Monarch brand. These are "value" spirits and are contract distilled by distilleries outside Oregon.

By the mid-1960s, the old distillery building could not handle the volume of products being processed and bottled. A much larger facility was constructed on the plain below Hood River, and with its completion in 1968, HRD ceased distilling altogether. The old distillery building was completely demolished in the late 1970s.

It would be another seventeen years before another licensed producer would operate a still in Oregon.

HRD has continued to add distilled-elsewhere spirits to its portfolio. Since 2000, the company has been bottling a number of Canadian whiskeys under the Pendleton label, and in 2014, it acquired Lucid Absinthe.

There have been two significant developments at HRD in the last several years. The first was the 2014 acquisition of Clear Creek Distillery in Portland, which will be discussed further in the next chapter. Worth mentioning here is a bottling of Clear Creek apple brandy carrying the Old Delicious label to commemorate HRD's eightieth anniversary. This was a limited release and was available only from HRD's new tasting room, which opened in 2015 and is located in downtown Hood River.

The second major development is the 2015 decision to resume distilling in Hood River. A 2,000-liter (528-gallon) capacity column still has been purchased from the German firm of Christian Carl, and a new building is being constructed to house it. Although not yet operational in mid-2016, the company will be using it to produce super-premium fruit-based vodka.[93]

Apart from HRD's activities, there isn't much else to mention for the 1934 to 1984 period. There was one additional distillery started about the same time as HRD. This was **Columbia Distillers** (DSP-OR-2) in Salem, which made a small range of fruit brandies and liqueurs. By 1939, the company had ceased distilling in order to concentrate on wine production and had renamed itself **Honeywood Winery**. It continues to operate under that name, producing wine from both grapes and other fruit.[94]

One noteworthy event was the 1943 acquisition of two Kentucky bourbon distilleries by the OLCC and its counterpart in Washington. Bourbon was in short supply during World War II, and the two states wanted to ensure bourbon-loving northwesterners would have an adequate supply. The Waterfill & Frasier distillery in Anchorage was purchased for $3,650,000 and the Shawhan distillery in Bardstown for $2,800,000.[95] After the war, the two distilleries were sold to private investors.

⸜⸝

Ted Pooley's father, Edward Pooley, died in Hood River in 1950 at age ninety-two.

Edward Lee McClain died in Los Angeles in 1954. He was sixty-seven. Edna, his daughter by his first wife, married and had one child, a daughter. Her family lives in Honolulu, Hawaii.

Albert William Peters remarried twice, with his final wife, Maude Bauman, surviving him. He died in Hood River in 1967 at age eighty-one. Maude died in 1980. His second daughter, Marguerite, had two daughters, one of whom, Jill Stanford, has provided invaluable information about the Peters, Pooley and McClain families.

Edwin Randolph "Ted" Pooley died in Hood River in 1977 at age ninety-one. Dorothy survived him by one year. War-widow daughter Barbara eventually remarried and had two more children. Before his death, Pooley had merged his fruit company with Duckwall Fruit, and the new company was known for a while as the Duckwall-Pooley Fruit Company; after Ted Pooley's death, the Duckwalls dropped the Pooley name. The house built by Ted Pooley in 1927 (designed by Portland architect Jamieson Parker) is still standing and appears to be in good condition.

Norwegian Spy

1 ½ ounces Clear Creek apple brandy (the two-year-old)
½ ounce apricot liqueur
¾ ounce apple cider
½ ounce lemon juice
2 dashes Angostura bitters
sparkling wine

Combine brandy, liqueur, cider, lemon juice and bitters and shake with ice. Strain into a tumbler with ice. Top with sparkling wine.

9

CLEAR CREEK

Stephen R. McCarthy was born in Seattle in 1943. His family had been in the Pacific Northwest for at least a couple of generations, having acquired orchard property near Hood River. The family lost the orchards during the Great Depression, and Steve's father moved to Seattle to find work. In 1950, the family moved to Myrtle Creek, Oregon, where the elder McCarthy took a job at a local sawmill. In the late 1950s, Steve McCarthy attended Roseburg High School, where he served as vice-president of the school's International Relations League, a club that, according to the 1960 school yearbook, endeavored "to promote interest in international understanding."

After graduation, Steve McCarthy enrolled in Reed College in Portland (other alumni of Reed include Steve Jobs, James Beard and McCarthy's wife, artist Lucinda Parker). With his interest in international subjects, in 1961 he took advantage of an exchange program with the University of Grenoble. Located in the foothills of the French Alps, Grenoble is a popular destination for those interested in winter sports and hosted the Winter Olympics in 1968. McCarthy joined in a number of these activities, including cross-country skiing. After returning from these outings, participants would warm themselves with a shot or two of spirit, with pear eau de vie being a popular choice. This was Steve McCarthy's first exposure to this particular spirit, and it soon became a favorite.[96]

Graduating from Reed in 1966, McCarthy attended law school at NYU, which he completed in 1969. He returned to Portland and married that same year. He practiced law for a couple years and then served as director of the Oregon State Public Interest Research group from 1972 to 1974 and director of TRIMET (the Portland area transit system) from 1974 to 1978.

Meanwhile, his father had acquired a company (Michaels of Oregon) that manufactured accessories for hunting firearms. The company was successful, and the McCarthy family used some of the profits to reacquire its Hood River orchard property. Steve McCarthy went to work for his father's company in 1978, and his activities included traveling to Europe to market the company's products. During these trips, he would make it a point to sample more eaux de vie (*eaux* is the plural of *eau*), not just those from pear but from other fruits as well. It was during this period that McCarthy learned that the Williams pear used in the European brandy was the same variety as the Bartlett pear grown by his family in Oregon.

Steve McCarthy had, by the early 1980s, acquired his father's company and significantly boosted its size and revenues but increasingly found himself drawn to the idea of starting a distillery. He visited Jörg Ruph, who founded St. George Distillery in 1982 (in Alameda, California) and offered to pay Ruph $75,000 ($172,000 in 2016 dollars) to teach him how to make seven different types of eau de vie.

The establishment of St. George in 1982 was facilitated by a significant change in the regulation of distilleries by the IRS, a change that was a necessary condition for the rise of the modern craft distilling movement. Until 1982, all distilleries, regardless of size, required the presence of a full-time IRS agent (known as a "storekeeper") who had exclusive access to all spirits in storage. If a prospective distillery operator projected production below a certain level, the IRS could not justify a full-time agent and would usually refuse to issue a license. In January 1982, the IRS underwent a major reorganization, one element of which was the elimination of storekeepers. This removed the primary obstacle to the establishment of small distilleries, and distillery operators now had unrestricted access to their own products.

In 1984, McCarthy purchased a building on the west side of Portland, at 1430 Northwest Twenty-Third Avenue, and began converting it into a distillery.

For the licensing for the distillery, the federal Bureau of Alcohol, Tobacco and Firearms proved "amazingly helpful" and assigned DSP-OR-6 to **Clear Creek Distillery**.[97] The Oregon Liquor Control Commission was cooperative as well but apparently wasn't optimistic about the distillery's prospects. "I don't think they took me seriously," said McCarthy. "Their attitude seemed to be, 'Oh sure, go ahead.'"

McCarthy ordered a $15,000 still from Arnold Holstein in Germany, the same type used by Ruph at St. George. The still, of 270-liter (70-gallon) capacity, arrived damaged and had to be returned. Its replacement did not arrive until the early summer of 1985, and although it was delivered in good condition, it was without instructions. Its assembly was a trial-and-error affair, assisted by Polaroid photographs being photocopied and faxed to Arnold Holstein, who would reply with an appropriate response ("Ja that is correct" or "Nein, that part is on upside-down").

After the still was assembled, a successful test run was performed using some Chardonnay. That autumn, a load of pears was brought in from Hood River, crushed, fermented and placed into the still, and the distillation run started. As the spirit began to emerge from the still, the funky head spirits were diverted, as was the watery tail, and those present sampled the heart. The group included Oregon winemaking pioneer David Lett, who, when he tried it, announced, "This is amazing."

The brandy was placed into large glass containers for several weeks and then bottled, being available for sale before the end of 1985. Portland-area gourmets, who had only recently discovered that some very fine wine was being produced not too far south of the city, were receptive to the distillery's product, and it was soon selling well enough to encourage McCarthy to order a second still. Realizing he'd need a diverse product line to attract distributors, he introduced apple brandy (aged for two years in French oak; some was set aside for longer aging), followed by kirsch (cherry eau de vie) and *framboise* (raspberry).

Success in his prior business had taught McCarthy the importance of networking, particularly with writers. He reached out to wine and spirits critics, and in February 1989, Frank Prial of the *New York Times* published "Oregon Original," an enthusiastic article about McCarthy and his products. Prial's column was syndicated and appeared in newspapers all over the country, and Clear Creek thereby gained national visibility.

By this time, McCarthy was fully committed to the distillery, having sold the firearm accessory company "for a boatload of money" in 1987. He put together a team of "very capable people" to assist in making and marketing the distillery's spirits and added new products to the line, such as grappa. The distillery had made an experimental batch back in the 1980s, when David Lett brought two garbage cans full of Muscat Ottonel pomace. The results were encouraging, and several varieties of grappa were introduced over the following years. Unlike most European brandies of this type, the pomace for which is produced from overpressed, inexpensive grapes ("Stuff

Steve McCarthy at the original Clear Creek facility, circa 1990. *Photo courtesy Clear Creek Distillery.*

I'd never let in the building," as McCarthy describes it), Clear Creek sources from local wineries that use good-quality grapes and processing techniques that leave behind a better grade of pomace (of course, it is pomace, and the distillery pays little to nothing for it).

The next spirit in the product line was McCarthy's single-malt whiskey. Steve and Lucinda McCarthy were vacationing in the British Isles during the early 1990s when he sampled some Lagavulin, a Scottish single malt from the island of Islay (pronounced *EYE-leh*). McCarthy liked the smoky, peaty flavor of the Lagavulin and decided to see if he could make something similar. This required compromising a principle the distillery had followed from the beginning: to source its raw materials locally (Oregon or Washington). There being no local source of peat-smoked barley malt, the only option was to import it from Scotland. This made for an expensive product, and letting it age the over eight years that a Scottish malt usually receives meant having a lot of capital tied up in the barrels, so McCarthy decided to bottle it at three years of age. Despite its youth, it was a critical success, with spirits reviewer Jim Murray usually giving a 95-point or higher rating in his annual *Whisky Bible*, and the semiannual releases of McCarthy's single malt sell out quickly, despite an over fifty-dollar price tag.

Two Oregon pioneers: David Lett of the Eyrie Vineyard (*left*) delivering *pomace* to Steve McCarthy of Clear Creek, circa 1990. *Courtesy Clear Creek Distillery.*

Another product introduced during the 1990s was the eight-year-old version of the apple brandy. Over the years, I'd sampled a number of calvados, the French equivalent, prior to purchasing a bottle of the Clear Creek. I've not bought any calvados since and consider the Clear Creek to be world class.

The 1990s also saw the introduction of a fruit-in-the-bottle expression of the pear eau de vie. This has been a traditional offering from a number of European producers (e.g., Massenez) and was suggested to McCarthy by a distributor. To create these, a bottle is slipped over a developing pear bud and secured with ties to higher branches. Only two thousand of these are set each year; not all survive to harvest, with some succumbing to natural breakage and others being used for target practice by Hood River–area nimrods.

The 2005–7 period was marked by a number of significant events for Clear Creek. In 2005, the distillery began introducing a line of liqueurs, which eventually included cranberry, blackberry, loganberry, raspberry, cassis, cherry and pear. These are made by macerating the fruit in unaged brandy (made of the same fruit when possible; i.e., the raspberry is made using the distillery's *framboise*), a method that produces purer and more natural aromas and flavors than that achieved by simply adding sugar and fruit concentrate to neutral spirit (which is how most liqueurs are produced).

In the spring of 2006, the distillery moved to its current location, 2389 Northwest Wilson Street in Portland. The new building allowed for the addition of two more stills: a secondhand one was acquired from Bonny Doon winery in California, and another was ordered new from Arnold Holstein. With these in place, production capacity was doubled.

In 2007, another highly complimentary article appeared in the *New York Times*, this one by Eric Asimov. Titled "An Orchard in a Bottle, at 80 Proof," the article reinforced the reputation created by the Prial article of 1989.

For most of the distillery's history, McCarthy had focused on two goals: learn how to make superior brandies of various types (every time a new type of fruit was selected there was a learning curve) and educate American drinkers regarding eau de vie and its place in the montage of foods and beverages available to the eclectic palate. To this end, McCarthy networked not only with writers and critics but also with distributors, restaurateurs and owners of high-end liquor stores.

Both of these goals had been largely achieved by 2008, and McCarthy turned his attention to the task of making Clear Creek a profitable business. Up until that time, the company had operated on a break-even basis, turning a small profit one year followed by a small loss the next. The ultimate goal was to make Clear Creek an attractive purchase for a potential new owner.

McCarthy turned seventy in 2013 and decided it was time to retire. He wanted Clear Creek to remain an Oregon-owned company, and the only potential same-industry purchaser large

Harvesting pears in the bottle for Clear Creek.
Courtesy Clear Creek Distillery.

enough to afford to buy the distillery was Hood River Distillers. He reached out to HRD, and negotiations were successfully concluded in early 2014.

To date, HRD has not made too many changes in the Clear Creek operation. One immediate benefit of newly available capital was the purchase of forty-five new barrels for brandy aging. Some operational efficiencies have been introduced, and the eaux de vie are now aged in stainless steel containers instead of glass. Some low-sales-volume products have been dropped, such as the Gewürztraminer grappa, and several other products are receiving new packaging. The McCarthy single malt is still made at Clear Creek but is now marketed as an HRD product.[98]

Currently, the Clear Creek product line includes six eaux de vie (pear, cherry, blue plum, Mirabelle plum, raspberry and Douglas fir—yes, you read that right; it's not actually distilled from Douglas fir but made by macerating buds in clear brandy), three aged brandies (two-year-old grape, two-year-old apple and eight-year-old apple), seven liqueurs (cranberry, blackberry, loganberry, raspberry, cassis, cherry and pear), four grappas (Muscat, Pinot Noir, Nebbiolo and Sangiovese) and the single-malt whiskey. The distillery employs ten people.

It is almost impossible to overestimate the historical significance of Clear Creek. Much as the Boston Beer Company (Samuel Adams) demonstrated in the beer industry, Clear Creek showed that even in a market dominated by large corporate manufacturers, a small, privately held producer could succeed. With a unique and innovative line of high-quality products, both companies established a firm place in their respective markets and, more importantly, paved the way for the hundreds of craft breweries and distilleries that followed (one significant debt owed to McCarthy by Oregon distillers is for his vigorous promotion of legislation that allows tasting rooms and direct sales to visitors).

Steve McCarthy says he would do it all over again; his only regret is that he didn't start ten years sooner. He also would have liked to have added a sour-mash whiskey (as in, a bourbon or straight rye) to the product line but never had time for that. He's currently enjoying his retirement and lives with

Steve McCarthy in 2016. *Photo by the author.*

his wife, Lucinda, and their cat in a beautifully restored home in an older Portland neighborhood.

As a final note, I think it's worth mentioning that Kitty McCarthy (the cat) was an active participant during my interview with Steve, offering a uniquely feline perspective. When the subject of flavored vodka came up, Kitty opined, "Most of it smells like cat pee anyway—and I'm an authority on that subject."

Eve's Temptation

2 ounces Clear Creek apple brandy (the two-year-old)
¾ ounce sweet vermouth, such as Carpano Antica Formula
¼ ounce Clear Creek eau de vie of Douglas fir
1 teaspoon Averna
1 twist lemon peel (garnish)

Stir liquids with ice. Strain into a chilled cocktail glass. Garnish with lemon peel.

Big Blue Plum

2 ounces Clear Creek blue plum eau de vie
1 ounce Midori liqueur
1 slice honeydew melon or lime (garnish)

Shake the eau de vie and liqueur with ice; strain into a martini glass. Garnish with melon or lime.

SECOND WAVE

I n the years following the founding of Clear Creek, an increasing number of entrepreneurs began distilling in Oregon. The 1980s saw one additional distiller, the 1990s added five more and another nineteen started during the first decade of the twenty-first century. Here are their stories.

EVE ATKINS

Seth Yorra was a classmate of Steve McCarthy's at Reed College, graduating in 1967 with a degree in German Theater. He went on to get a master's of art from the University of Iowa in directing and dramaturgy (this last term defined as "the theory and practice of dramatic composition") in 1970 and then entered law school at Golden Gate University in San Francisco in 1978, receiving a degree three years later.

Somewhere along the line, he met and married Diane Harrison, who was also involved in the performing arts. Their first child, Marie, was born in 1980 and a second, Michelle, in 1983.

What motivated the Yorras to get into the distilling business? Seth Yorra provided this explanation:

> I chose that enterprise because we wanted to bring our children up close
> to the soil. After more than a year of looking, we found an orchard in

Hood River, where we were looking because of the excellent terroir in the wind-washed slope of the upper Hood River Valley. My father and I had independently traveled to cognac country in France, and when we put all of the experience together, it seemed that distilling in Oregon was inevitable.[99]

The Yorras purchased the farm and in 1989 founded Eve Atkins Distillery (named after Seth Yorra's mother). They acquired an Arnold Holstein still, converted the barn into a distillery and began making fruit brandy from pears, apples (aged and—unusual—a *eau de vie*), blueberries and cherries. The brandy was sold under the Marichelle label, the name being a combination of their daughters' names.

Seth Yorra was splitting his time between the distillery, his law practice in Boston and activity in Europe, with Diane and their daughters remaining in Hood River. Although Seth was always there in the autumn to perform fermenting and distilling, and temporary help was hired to assist Diane with her part of the operation, an article written in 1991 by Ron Cowan of the Gannett News Service suggests that Diane was hoping to transfer more of the work to experienced employees, quoting her as saying, "The idea is to have very expert trained labor. We need to spend our time on marketing, advertising."

Of course, finding "very expert trained labor" in those days was a tall order. The craft distilling movement was in its nascent phase, and finding an experienced distiller to work in Hood River was probably not possible.

The Yorras succeeded in making a good product; Marichelle was well received by critics and successful in tasting competitions. The distillery was not, however, a commercial success, and by the end of 1997, both the distilling operation and the Yorras' marriage had come to an end. The property was put up for sale, with an asking price of $850,000, which included (according to a February 18, 1998 *Register-Guard* article) "a 90-year-old English craftsman style house and grounds, 20 acres of orchards, a barn that has been converted into a distillery with a German-made pot still and lots of barrels of brandy." The property was eventually sold, with the new owners not interested in continuing the distilling operation. The still was sold to a distillery outside Oregon and, according to Yorra, "was misused and allowed to explode." It's not known what became of all the brandy.

Bittersweet Memory

1 ½ ounces Big Bottom apple brandy (unaged)
3 ounces ruby red grapefruit juice
5 dashes orange bitters

Shake with ice; strain into a martini glass.

BRANDY PEAK

Radford Nowlin (who prefers to go by his initials, RL) was born in Texas in 1921. After serving in the navy during World War II, he received a degree in chemical engineering.[100] In 1947, he was working for Schenleys Wine Division at the Roma Winery in Fresno, which had just taken delivery of a brandy still from the Oscar Krenz company. The still was not working properly, and representatives from the manufacturer were unable to correct the problem. Nowlin was able to solve it and subsequently received a job offer from Oscar Krenz. He worked for the company for the next several years, engineering stills for various California brandy producers, and then accepted the chief engineer position with E.&J. Gallo in 1956. In 1961, he started his own company, L&A Engineering, which produced stills as well as other equipment for chemical processing. He sold the company in 1983.

In 1984, Nowlin received the James F. Guymon Award from the American Society of Enology and Viticulture. During the society's annual meeting that year, he presented a paper—"Distilled Beverages: A Challenge for Tomorrow"—that detailed the issues associated with distilling fruit brandies.

In 1993, he and his son David began construction of a distillery near Brookings, Oregon. Brandy Peak Distillery (DSP-OR-11) became operational in 1994, with its first product being pear eau de vie. Over the next several years, a number of products were introduced, including grape brandy, grappa (their mixed-varietal grappa is one of the few that I've actually liked), blackberry liqueur and an aged pear brandy. This last is unusual, as most pear brandy is sold as unaged eau de vie. It is five years old and very good, and I've always had a bottle on hand since first trying it in 2013.

The distillery's two stills were designed by the senior Nowlin, constructed by his former company, and are unique in being wood-fired.

They are both of four-hundred-gallon capacity but are not usually filled with any more than two hundred gallons of fermented material. They don't look like most stills I've seen; in fact, they look more like furnaces than anything else.

The to-be-aged brandies are put into a solera, a fractional blending system consisting of a series of barrels. After the barrel containing the oldest brandy is partially drained for to-be-bottled brandy, it's topped off from the barrel containing the next-oldest brandy and so on. Once the youngest barrel is partially emptied, it's topped off with freshly distilled spirit. The result is a more consistent product, and over time, the brandy becomes progressively richer (the Alvear company in Spain has a sherry solera that's been in use since 1927; the wine it produces is phenomenal). The grape brandy takes about six years to work its way through the solera; the pear about five.

Brandy Peak has never offered any more than seven or eight products at any given time, but concentrating on only a few has yielded spirits that have garnered numerous awards.

David Nowlin stoking one of the wood-fired stills. *Photo courtesy Brandy Peak Distillery.*

The distillery itself sits halfway up a mountain northeast of Brookings, nestled in a small opening in the forest. There is no white-lettered blue sign on Highway 101, nor any signs on the road that winds up the distillery. If you want to visit, you need to first locate it on a map and print out the directions (the distillery's website warns against relying on GPS).

R.L. Nowlin retired some years ago. Son David continues to operate the distillery, which has established itself as a producer of first-rate brandy.

Pearzerac

1 teaspoon Absinthe
3 dashes Peychaud's Bitters
½ tablespoon simple syrup
2 ounces Brandy Peak Aged Pear Brandy
1 twist lemon peel (garnish)

Add the absinthe to a chilled Old-Fashioned or rocks glass, roll around to coat interior, dump excess. Stir bitters, syrup and brandy with ice; strain into the glass. Garnish with lemon peel.

BENDISTILLERY

Jim Bendis was born in Akron, Ohio, in 1960. His family moved to Florida while he was still a boy, and he received an associate's degree in business from the University of Florida in 1980. He went west and eventually enrolled at the University of Oregon, receiving a bachelor's degree in marketing in 1982. He moved to Bend, where he worked as an advertising executive for a local television station.[101]

Bendis is a runner, and in 1995, while running through a patch of western juniper (*Juniperus occidentalis*), it occurred to him that a locally produced gin would fit right in with the fine wines and beers being made in the Pacific Northwest. He started the process of getting federal approval (eventually receiving DSP-OR-14) and established Bendistillery in 1995.

Although Bendis had originally planned to make only gin, local liquor store owners suggested he produce vodka as well. Like Hood River Distillers, Bendis purchased neutral spirit from large producers, diluting it to beverage strength with local water (most of which originates as meltwater from the nearby Cascades). The gin was made by steeping juniper berries in the spirit, which is then filtered to remove some of the color. Unlike most gins, no "botanicals" (herbs and spices) are used, with only the juniper providing flavor to the gin.

The distillery also makes a number of flavored vodkas. Because these obtain their flavors via infusion, rather than by the simple addition of flavoring, they are labeled "infused" and are classified as "distilled specialty spirits" by the IRS TTB, a category for whose creation Bendis lobbied.

The vodka and gin are sold under the Crater Lake brand; the distillery's products have also been sold under other labels, most being for companies that contracted with Bendistillery to produce it for them (about 20 percent of Bendistillery's production is for other companies).

Bendis had obtained a license to distill and acquired a small (twenty-five-gallon capacity) still for running off experimental batches of spirits. One of the first of these was a whiskey produced in 1996. Bendis had spent time with the head brewer at Deschutes Brewery in Bend and learned about the malts and grains used in the brewery's Black Butte porter. He worked up a similar mash (without hops), fermented it and ran it through the still, eventually producing about eight gallons of whiskey and putting it into a small oak barrel to see how it would age.

By 2010, the company was successful enough to acquire new property northwest of Bend and construct a new distillery. The facility occupies twenty-four acres, and barley and rye are grown on the property. There is abundant wild juniper growing both on and around the property. A medium capacity still (160 gallons) was acquired in 2011, supplemented by a large one (450 gallons) in 2014 (this last still is from Artisan Still Design and is a beautiful piece of equipment).

With these new resources have come additions to the product line. The first was an Estate gin introduced in 2013. Made from grain grown on the distillery property, it's redistilled after being infused with locally harvested juniper berries, and then given six to twelve weeks of barrel aging (such aging is unusual for a gin).

Shortly thereafter, a rye whiskey was introduced. Not having sufficient capacity to distill all of this itself, Bendistillery obtained unaged high-proof rye whiskey from Midwest Grain Products (MGP) in Indiana, aged it for a year in barrels of Oregon oak, diluted it with local water and bottled it. Whether it qualified as an Oregon product is debatable, but the point became moot at the end of 2014 when Bendistillery began distilling rye whiskey in its new high-capacity still. This whiskey is 100 percent rye (the MGP was 95 percent) and is aged fourteen to sixteen months.

The distillery had been producing a small amount of its own rye whiskey since 2013, using the medium capacity still. The first of this, three years old and bottled as Crater Lake Reserve Rye, began shipping on June 15, 2016.

In 2012, Jim Bendis and Gary Fish (owner of Deschutes Brewery) sampled some of the Black Butte whiskey made in the small still in 1996. By this time, it was sixteen years old, and the proof had increased to 160 (this can happen under the right climatic conditions). Bendis describes it as "amazing." Bendis and Fish agreed to collaborate on a Black Butte whiskey, with the brewery producing a hop-free version of the beer and Bendistillery distilling it into whiskey, aging and bottling it. The first release should be before the end of 2016; I, for one, am eagerly anticipating this.

Although from 1996 through 2010 Bendistillery was considered by some to be nothing more than a bottling company, relying on spirits distilled elsewhere, since 2011 it has been introducing products made entirely on site. It's a welcome development and one that deserves recognition.

MIDWEST GRAIN PRODUCTS (MGP)

MGP is not an Oregon distillery, but many Oregon companies sell MGP whiskey as their own product, and this seems as good a place as any to mention this. MGP owns the old Seagrams distillery in Lawrenceburg, Indiana, which is one of the largest whiskey distilleries in the United States. MGP sells no brands of its own but supplies various types of whiskies to producers across the country, not just in Oregon. The Oregon producers who bottle MGP whiskey will be identified in due course.

RANSOM

Tad Seestedt was born in Michigan in 1965, but spent most of his early years on a farm in Upstate New York. In the late 1980s, he visited Oregon, liked the climate and decided he'd like to pursue a career in winemaking. He began making wine in 1993 and started his own winery in 1999.[102]

Seestedt had also developed an interest in distilling, which he saw as a natural extension of winemaking. He started Ransom Spirits (DSP-OR-15) in 1997, using space rented from Honeywood Winery in Salem (you may recall that Honeywood started as a distillery back in the 1930s). By 1999, he'd transferred the operation to leased space in Corvallis, in the building that currently houses Taylor Street Ovens on Ninth Street. His first still was a Hoga unit (a Portuguese company) of about sixty-gallon capacity, and his first products were grappa and eau de vie. He later supplemented it with a larger still of two-hundred-gallon capacity.

Distilling was a seasonal activity, taking place during the three months following grape and fruit harvests. For the rest of the year, the distillery was idle. Consequently, Seestedt was receptive when Christian Krogstad and Lee Medoff approached him in 2004 with a time-sharing proposal. Krogstad and Medoff, who had worked at McMenamins for many years, were interested in

Seestedt's Hoga Still, photographed at House Spirits in 2010. *Photo by the author.*

producing vodka, gin and whiskey and hoped to save some time and money by piggybacking onto an existing operation. They and Seestedt approached the IRS TTB and were surprised by an "amazingly cooperative" response. The agency issued the first-ever permit for joint proprietorship of a distillery, with Ransom occupying and using it for three months of the year and House Spirits (Krogstad and Medoff's company) using it for the other nine.

Krogstad and Medoff realized better accommodations were needed for both their operation and Seestedt's. They found a suitable space in east Portland and moved their operation there in early 2006. They acquired a four-hundred-gallon steam-heated still, which is still in use at House Spirits. In 2007, Seestedt moved his operation to the Portland facility.

Seestedt never intended this to be anything more than a temporary home for his distilling. His goal was to consolidate his winemaking and distilling on a single site, and in 2008, he purchased a forty-acre farm near Sheridan in Yamhill County. An existing three-thousand-square-foot building was converted into a distillery, and a new four-thousand-square-foot winery was built next door. He sold his existing stills to House Spirits, having acquired a 265-gallon Prulho cognac still. This still had been manufactured in 1978 and imported for use in a California brandy distillery, but it had never been installed. Seestedt later supplemented this still with an even larger Prulho unit (660 gallons) that was too large to house inside the distillery building and was installed just outside its walls.

By this time, Seestedt had become interested in grain-based spirits and in 2009 introduced his Old Tom gin. Developed with assistance from spirits historian David Wondrich, the product is a re-creation of the style of gin most popular during the mid-nineteenth century. Made from barley (malted and unmalted) and corn and given six to twelve months of barrel aging, Old Tom received high marks from spirits reviewers and developed a solid fan base, eventually becoming Ransom's bestselling product.

Ransom has also introduced a number of whiskeys, the first being WhipperSnapper Oregon Spirit Whiskey. Spirit whiskey, as defined by the IRS TTB's standards of identity, is essentially vodka with a minimum whiskey content of only 5 percent, but WhipperSnapper contains considerably more than that. Seestedt chose this category to avoid the requirement for aging in new, charred barrels, which he feels has too great an effect on the character of the spirit. Being first and foremost a winemaker, Seestedt wants the aroma and flavor of the original materials to come through in the final product, and using "neutral" (uncharred and/or already used) barrels achieves this goal. WhipperSnapper is best thought of as an American analog to blended

Tad Seestedt of Ransom Distillery with one of his stills. *Photo by the author.*

Scotch and Irish whiskey and is considerably better than the typical blended American whiskey.

The Henry du Yore line of whiskeys are traditional American types (as in, bourbon and rye) and are blends of whiskey sourced from eastern distilleries and whiskey distilled at Ransom. The Henry du Yore bourbon is currently not in production, with a rye whiskey being the current offering.

Ransom's flagship whiskey is the Emerald, another re-creation of a nineteenth-century spirit, in this case Irish whiskey, using a recipe discovered by Wondrich. Despite having less than four years of barrel time, this is a very good whiskey (and considering its price of seventy dollars, it needs to be).

Today, the Ransom product line is dominated by gins and whiskeys, with the Gewürztraminer grappa being the only remaining fruit-based spirit.

A Sweeter Egress

A variation on "(This way to) the Egress," reversing the proportions of lemon juice and apricot liqueur.

2 ounces Ransom Old Tom Gin
¾ ounce Marie Brizard Apry Apricot Liqueur
½ ounce lemon juice

Shake with ice; strain into a chilled cocktail glass.

McMENAMINS: EDGEFIELD AND CORNELIUS PASS

McMenamins is a chain of taverns, brewpubs and hotels with over sixty locations in Oregon and Washington. Founded by brothers Mike and Brian McMenamin during the early 1980s, the company began brewing its own beer in 1985 and started its own winery in 1990. With this "we'll make our own" philosophy, it was only natural that it would start distilling as well, and in 1995, the company began the process of establishing a distillery. The chain's Edgefield location was selected as the site for the distillery, and the conversion of a storage barn was begun in 1997. License DSP-OR-16 was assigned by the IRS TTB, and a sixty-six-gallon still was purchased from Arnold Holstein.[103]

St. George Spirits distiller Lance Winters was hired as a consultant, but the McMenamins team also received advice from Booker Noe (master distiller at Jim Beam Bourbon) and Hubert Germain-Robin (whose distillery in Ukiah, California, produces brandy that rivals the finest from Cognac). During this period Germain-Robin happened to be visiting France and came across a for-sale still in Cognac. It was one hundred years old but still perfectly usable, so despite its being too large for the Edgefield distillery building, McMenamins purchased it, brought it to Oregon and put it in storage.

Hoping to get a jump on brandy production, McMenamins sent some of its Pinot Noir wine to the RMS[104] distillery in 1995, 1996 and 1997. A total of thirteen barrels were filled; seven remain. First released in 2008 as Alambic 13 Brandy and still labeled as such, the youngest is currently over eighteen years old. I sampled some of this while visiting Edgefield in mid-2016; it is, in a word, phenomenal (it may not have been distilled in Oregon, but the grapes were grown here, the wine was made here and the brandy was aged here, and it thus has a better claim to being produced in Oregon than some spirits that state that on their label).

The Edgefield distillery began production in 1998, with its first release being Safari, an unaged brandy made from Semillon. This was followed by

McMenamins Distillery at Cornelius Pass. A 120-year-old still in a 160-year-old barn. How cool is that? *Photo by the author.*

Longshot, a similar brandy made from Syrah and still in the product line (although it now receives a year of barrel age). In 1999, an unaged version of Hogshead malt whiskey was introduced, followed six months later by an aged version; this latter now receives three years of barrel age.

By 2006, when James Whelan became distiller, the product line included six spirits. Adding additional spirits meant running the still in multiple shifts, and in the years since, three additional distillers have been added, along with a brewer dedicated to the distilling operation. At the end of 2015, another still was acquired, a 270-gallon unit from Global Stainless Systems, to supplement the hardworking Arnold Holstein unit.

The Edgefield line now includes four brandies, four liqueurs, three whiskeys, two rums and a gin. The Pot Still brandy, currently a blend of eleven-year-old Pinot Noir and nine-year-old Semillon brandy, is a personal favorite of mine.

In 2011, McMenamins decided to convert into a distillery one of the barns at its Cornelius Pass Roadhouse facility. The barn, built in 1855, was large enough to accommodate the 160-gallon capacity antique Cognac still as well as provide storage for a fair number of barrels. Longtime McMenamins employee Bart Hance was tapped to become head distiller, and he and distiller Arthur Price have been producing rum, liqueur and an as-yet-unreleased rye whiskey. The new distillery was assigned license DSP-OR-15043 (for its own inscrutable reasons, the IRS TTB jumped from DSP-OR-22 to DSP-OR-15000 in 2005 and from DSP-OR-15053 to DSP-OR-20000 in 2011).

The 120-year-old still seems right at home in the 160-year-old barn, and the combination conveys a marvelous and unique impression of antiquity (you'd never guess they've been together for only five years). If you're planning a tour of Oregon distilleries, Cornelius Pass should definitely be on your list.

ROGUE

Rogue is one of the larger brewing companies in Oregon and is known for both an extensive line of quality beer and for the quirky sense of humor expressed in its written content and its product names (for example, the company describes its products as being made with "free range" water).

Sometime around 2002, the company decided to start distilling. As near as I can determine, the first license obtained (DSP-OR-19) was for the Rogue

Distillery and Public House in Portland. Here a very small still (I estimate it at twenty-five-gallon capacity) was installed behind glass to allow viewing by patrons. The first spirits produced, in 2003, were various styles of rum; today, any number of "experimental" spirits are distilled there.

In 2005, Rogue obtained a distilling license for its Newport plant (DSP-OR-15007), acquired a bigger still and began producing rum in quantity. Soon after that, Dead Guy Whiskey was introduced; this is made from the ale of the same name. It's aged only thirty days and tastes like it, being quite raw. Later a single-malt whiskey was introduced; its initial release was only three months old. The latest whiskeys are a chipotle flavored one and a rye; two vodkas (one being the Voodoo Bacon Maple), two "spruce" gins (one is pink) and two dark rums round out the line.

Many of these have not been well received (the hazelnut-flavored rum has been compared to "moldering gingerbread"), and you cannot help but wonder if Rogue is making a sincere effort. It's easy to believe that the whole thing is just for fun. There's nothing wrong with that, I guess, but I can't help but feel disappointed that the company is not realizing its potential. It's large enough that it could afford to delay its return-on-investment and age its whiskeys longer than any other Oregon producer; instead, it ages them for less time than nearly all of them.

HOUSE SPIRITS

As related in the section for Ransom, Christian Krogstad and Lee Medoff entered into a joint proprietorship with Tad Seestedt in 2004, with the Corvallis distillery operating as House Spirits (DSP-OR-21) for nine months out of the year. Using neutral spirits sourced from a distillery outside Oregon, the partners began making vodka, gin and aquavit (aquavit—or "akvavit"—can be thought of as a Scandinavian sort of gin, with caraway replacing juniper as the main flavoring ingredient). The gin and aquavit were made by steeping the appropriate flavoring materials in neutral spirit and then redistilling in one of Seestedt's stills.[105]

Both partners lived in Portland, and the commute to Corvallis had to be an onerous one. At the end of 2005, Krogstad and Medoff acquired a two-thousand-square-foot facility located at 2025 Southeast Seventh Avenue in Portland. A new four-hundred-gallon-capacity still was purchased, which allowed the partners to significantly ramp up production. The facility also included a tasting room—the Apothecary Room—which was done in a traditional style, with wood paneling and shelving.

Rum was added to the product line, as was a straight-malt whiskey. The latter was made from unsmoked malt but differed from Irish whiskey in that it was aged in a new barrel with a charred interior (required by the use of the word *straight*). Aged for about two and a half years, a 375-milliliter bottle sold for a little over forty-five dollars.

I visited House Spirits in January 2010, sampling all of the then current products and finding them to be good examples of their respective types. I liked the malt whiskey but felt that it was a bit pricey for what it was.

From the very beginning, its bestselling product was Aviation Gin, which accounted for 80 percent of its production. In 2011, House Spirits acquired an even larger still (seven hundred gallons) that was to be used exclusively for gin production. The smaller still would be used for the various other products.

In mid-2010, Lee Medoff left to start his own distillery, Bull Run. The House Spirits vodka, which had been labeled Medoyeff, was renamed Volstead after the federal law that implemented Prohibition in 1920.

The popularity of Aviation Gin continued to rise and demand exceeded the company's ability to produce it. Krogstad lined up some new investors and in early 2015 began construction of a fourteen-thousand-square-foot facility located at 65 Southeast Washington Street. Opening in November 2015, the new distillery is sleek and modern, the antithesis of the one at McMenamins's Cornelius Pass, and the tasting room is likewise aesthetically distant from the one at the previous House Spirits location (so much so that the oak barrels that sit in the room seem totally out of place). In addition to having the capacity to produce considerably more gin, there is an obvious commitment to boosting whiskey production, with a grain silo capable of holding seventy-five thousand pounds of malted barley and a three-thousand-gallon-capacity whiskey still. This still is a genuine pot still, of a similar type used by Scottish malt whiskey producers, but differs from most of those by being almost completely surrounded by the stainless steel jacket required by the steam heating system. This still, manufactured by Vendome, the Louisville, Kentucky company that makes stills for the big whiskey distillers in that state, is unquestionably the largest in Oregon and is claimed to be the largest operating whiskey still west of the Mississippi.

To operate all this equipment, House Spirits currently employs about twenty-five people, as well as a sophisticated computer system. Indeed, the

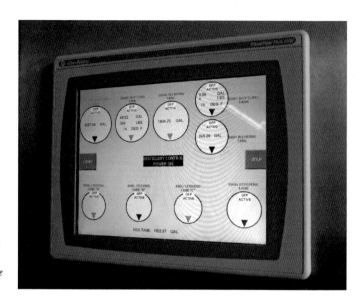

These days at House Spirits, the computers are in charge. *Photo by the author.*

entire operation is very high-tech, and I can honestly say I've never in my life seen that much stainless steel in one place.

House Spirits has opened a tasting room at Portland International Airport, and this is the retirement home for Tad Seestedt's original Hoga still.

The current product line includes two gins (an Old Tom version of Aviation was added at the end of 2015), vodka, aquavit (both unaged and a version that spends ten to twelve months in a barrel), malt whiskey (now named Westward Oregon Straight Malt Whiskey and aged thirty-eight to forty months) and a coffee liqueur.

Scandinavian Evening

1½ ounces Krogstad Krestlig Aquavit
¼ ounce St. Elizabeth Allspice Dram liqueur
¾ ounce lemon juice
½ ounce simple syrup
½ ounce club soda

Shake all ingredients, except soda, with ice; strain into ice-filled cocktail glass. Top with soda water, and garnish with a lemon wedge.

The three-thousand-gallon whiskey still at House Spirits. *Photo by the author.*

NEW DEAL

Tom Burkleaux and Matthew Vanwinkle opened New Deal Distillery in 2004. Its initial products were vodka and several liqueurs. For its first few years of operation, Burkleaux and Vanwinkle's starting point for all of these was purchased neutral spirit. This they would redistill in order to eliminate the medicinal alcohol aromas that often characterize commodity neutral spirit (other non-distilling producers filter it for the same reason). They acquired a number of stills, none of which were very large capacity, but according to Tom Burkleaux, the real production bottleneck was their fermentation setup, which was of insufficient capacity and used electrical heating. In 2012, they purchased a building at 900 Southeast Salmon Street in Portland that had not only more square footage but also a high enough ceiling to accommodate a good size column still; plus it would allow steam heating for the fermentation tanks. A new, larger-capacity still was purchased from Christian Carl of Germany, and this, when operating with its columns, enables New Deal to produce its own vodka from grain. Purchased neutral spirit is still used in its lower-priced vodka (Portland 88), but the vodka carrying the distillery name is made from Oregon wheat.[106]

New Deal produces two gins, the No. 1 and the 33. Both emphasize juniper and lack the usual spice and herbal botanicals. The 33 is made using a juniper-filled basket suspended in the still; the hot vapors pass through the basket and extract flavor on the way. The No. 1 is made by steeping juniper berries in neutral spirit and redistilling in a custom still.

The other standard offerings include three liqueurs (coffee, ginger and bitter chocolate), as well as a pepper-infused vodka.

The distillery also offers the Distiller's Workshop series of small batch spirits. These are typically whiskeys and rums, both aged and unaged.

DOLMEN

Anders Johansen was born into a farming family in 1958. The farm, near McMinnville, included among its activities honey production, and when Anders became a home-brewer during his twenties, he was making mead as well as beer. His interest in the fermented honey beverage was partly grounded in boyhood readings of Viking sagas (mead being the favorite quaff of Beowulf and his buds), and he continued experimenting with it even after becoming a professional brewer.

Sometime around 2004, he decided to try distilling a batch. Pleased with the result, he decided to try commercial production and started Dolmen Distillery (DSP-OR-15000) in 2005. The small distillery, located on his father's farm, produced only one product, that being Worker Bee. Essentially a honey-based eau de vie, the eighty-proof spirit was slightly sweet and featured a subtle honey character.

Worker Bee was never produced in large quantities or well distributed (only two liquor stores in Portland carried it), and Johansen ceased production in 2010. He'd already taken another brewing job (with Southern Oregon Brewing in Medford) and in recent years has been offering consulting services to those attempting commercial mead production. He's kept both his federal and state distilling licenses active and, if he wanted to, could resume production at any time.

SIDE POCKET

Side Pocket Foods was founded in 1998 by siblings Jeff and Megan Myers. Located in Cottage Grove, the company spawned Side Pocket Distilling (DSP-OR-15002) in 2005, with their father, William, at the helm. The company was not licensed to do any distilling and was instead obtaining spirits from other companies and bottling them as its own products. Its best-known brand was Support Her, an "ultra-premium" (thirty-five-dollar) vodka. For each bottle sold, Side Pocket claimed to donate five dollars to breast cancer research and treatment.[107]

IRS auditors took note of some filing discrepancies, and agents arrived in 2012 with search warrants in hand. In the course of searching the premises, an unlicensed still was discovered; it seems that the company had been distilling brandy for a number of local wineries. To make matters worse, testing of the spirits produced by this still revealed high lead levels, usually a sign that the still had been constructed using lead-based solder.

In addition to operating the illegal still, it was determined that Side Pocket owed $879,000 in back taxes. The company was fined this amount, and William Myers was sentenced to one year in prison. Side Pocket Foods was permanently closed.[108]

What is noteworthy about the Side Pocket story is that what the company was doing—claiming to not be distilling but actually doing so—is the reverse of the much more usual case. It's a disturbingly frequent occurrence, both in Oregon and elsewhere, to find producers who claim to be distilling but actually are not.

NORTHWEST

Northwest Distillery (2005, DSP-OR-15005) produces flavored vodka using purchased neutral spirit.

INDIO

Indio Spirits (DSP-OR-15006) was chartered by John Ufford in 2004. Ufford had previously worked at McMenamins, overseeing their alcoholic beverage program, but the company's lack of interest in vodka led him to start his own enterprise. In 2005, he purchased a still and began making his own spirits, but after a couple years, he realized this was not cost-effective, particularly for vodka, and switched to using purchased neutral spirit.

In 2007, the operation moved from southeast Portland to Cottage Grove and co-located with Side Pocket Distillery in order to take advantage of its ready supply of neutral spirit. After Side Pocket's demise in 2012, Indio moved back to Portland. In addition to infused (flavored) vodka, the company also produces gin and spiced rum. Canadian whiskey is imported, given additional aging and sold as Snake River Stampede, and MGP rye whiskey is aged and sold as James Oliver Rye.[109]

DUNDEE HILLS

Torii Mor Winery is one of many Oregon wineries that include a fortified dessert wine among their products. In the past, most of these would contract with a distillery to convert a quantity of their table wine into the brandy required to make the fortified wine. Clear Creek had been available for this until 2005 or so but demand for its own products squeezed out the contract distilling (as mentioned above, Side Pocket's attempt to pick up some of this business is one of the reasons it got into trouble). With the unavailability of outside distilleries, a number of wineries started distilling their own brandy, and Torii Mor was the first of these, registering Dundee Hills Distillery (DSP-OR-15009) in 2006.

Until 2014, all the brandy was used for the winery's Syrah port, but in that year, they decided to bottle some. Made from Pinot Noir, the brandy spends about ten months in Hungarian oak barrels before being bottled. It's available at the winery's tasting room in Dundee; supposedly, a quantity is sold to the OLCC, but I don't find it on the agency's product list.

With the 2015 vintage, Torii Mor produced some grappa from Pinot Noir pomace. Still resting in stainless steel tanks at the time of this writing (July 2016), it will probably be available before the end of 2016.[110]

INTEGRITY SPIRITS

Integrity Spirits (DSP-OR-15012) was started in 2007 by Kieran Sienkiewicz and Rich Phillips. Sienkiewicz claims to have been inspired by the homemade still operated by Hawkeye Pierce on the television show *M*A*S*H*. He'd worked as a distiller at the Rogue Distillery & Public House before partnering with Phillips. The two acquired an Arnold Holstein still, along with a supplemental column for distilling neutral spirit. The distillery was located in east Portland, in the area that was to become known as Distillery Row.

Absinthe, the wormwood-flavored liqueur of notorious legend, became legal again in the United States in 2007, and Integrity's Trillium was the second American-made absinthe on the market. Trillium was followed by 12 Bridges gin and Lovejoy vodka.

The company closed in 2012, perhaps partly because of the unfavorable economics associated with distilling its own neutral spirit. Rich Phillips is currently trying to get back into the business under the name Affinity Spirits.

ARTISAN SPIRITS

Artisan Spirits (DSP-OR-15013) was founded in 2007 by three partners, Erik Martin, Ryan Csansky and Shane Thatcher. The partners wanted to distill their own vodka, despite the questionable economics. Two were produced, Martin Ryan, which was made from Syrah grapes, and Apia, which was made from honey. The distillery was another one located in Portland's Distillery Row.

The company closed in 2010. Martin and Csansky went on to form the Martin Ryan Distilling Company and produce Aria gin (see chapter 12).

DISTILLED IN OREGON

CASCADE PEAK

Cascade Peak Spirits (DSP-OR-15014) was started in 2007 by Diane Paulson and David Eliasen. Located in Ashland, the distillery was the first in Oregon to be organic certified, and its first two products were Organic Nation vodka and gin. The partners had acquired an Arnold Holstein still equipped with columns, but it's been reported that its production was supplemented by neutral spirit purchased from a Midwest distillery. The company introduced Oldfield rye whiskey in 2012.

Cascade Peak closed in 2014.

HIGHBALL

Highball Distillery (DSP-OR-15015) was another southeast Portland distillery. In 2007, partners Michael Klinglesmith and Michael Heavenor took over the space recently vacated by Indio Spirits and set out to create the most environmentally friendly distillery in Oregon. A very large custom still was constructed, one that was heated by electricity provided by wind power. The distillery's vodka, Elemental, was produced from organic wheat grown by local farmers. By all accounts, it was good vodka, but it needed to be, considering its thirty-five-dollar price tag.

In 2010, the lease on the building expired and the owner was unwilling to renew. The two Michaels were unable to find an affordable space large enough to accommodate their still, and the company ceased operation.

VINN

For several generations, the Ly family lived in Vietnam making baijiu from rice, but when that country and China had their little dustup in 1978, the Vietnamese government expelled many resident ethnic Chinese. Phan Ly, his wife and their five children eventually ended up in Oregon in 1979. Ly operated a series of Chinese restaurants over the next thirty years but in 2008 decided he wanted to resume distilling, so he closed his Wilsonville restaurant and started Vinn Distillery (DSP-OR- 15018) in that same city.[111]

Initially, the company was producing both baijiu and mijiu, the latter being Chinese rice wine. The Vinn version of this was fortified with a little baijiu, and this put it into a category not recognized by either the OLCC or the TTB, which ultimately caused its withdrawal from the market in 2012.

Rice cookers at Vinn. On Tuesdays, these and four others are running nonstop. *Photo by the author.*

The column still at Vinn, formerly used at Artisan Spirits. *Photo by the author.*

Most of the stills used by Vinn are simple pot stills. These started life as forty-gallon stainless steel stockpots but were converted into stills by a local welder. When Ly decided to add vodka to the lineup, it was discovered that these stills, like most pot stills, could not produce neutral spirit. Nine successive passes through the still brought the spirit to only 93 percent ABV, still short of the required 95 percent. Fortunately, the small column still originally used at Artisan Spirits had just become available, so Vinn acquired this to produce its vodka. Later a blackberry liqueur was introduced, using the vodka as its base.

The most recent addition to the Vinn lineup is a whiskey. This originated as an experiment; baijiu was put into a number of small barrels and allowed to age for a year. It's an interesting spirit; the aroma is a bit like that of dark rum, and the flavor is, well, unique.

Vinn is very much a family operation. Phan and his wife are mostly retired now, with the five children (all over forty) running the operation. All of them have day jobs, but Tuesday is "distillery day," and that's when things are happening. I visited Vinn on a Tuesday, and it was bustling with activity. Eight commercial rice cookers were steaming away, and cooked rice was being cooled down prior to being placed into fermenting tubs along with yeast and *Aspergillus* enzyme. The fermentation is a lengthy process, lasting one month for the rice destined to become vodka and six for that destined to become baijiu. Once fermentation is complete, the rice wine is put into the appropriate still. After distillation, the vodka is filtered, while the baijiu is placed into large tanks and allowed to settle.

Future products include a 106-proof baijiu (the current one is 80) and an Asian-style gin (still being "tweaked"). Vinn will also be experimenting with a liqueur made from black rice.

Spritzer by Joe

¾ ounce Vinn Baijiu
¾ ounce St. Germain liqueur
¾ ounce lemon juice
¾ ounce lime juice
I teaspoon simple syrup
I splash Sprite

Shake all ingredients, except Sprite, with ice; strain into ice-filled cocktail glass. Top with Sprite, and garnish with a lemon wedge.

LIL' BIT

The title for most mysterious distillery in Oregon goes to Lil' Bit Distilling (DSP-OR-15020). Founded by Romanian immigrant Mihai Talvan, it's housed in a purpose-built 3,200-square-foot building in Woodburn. The building was designed by Deca Architecture, which describes it as being designed to "hold 10 copper pot stills that will be visible to entering visitors through a large window. The stills are also referenced in the exterior materials, which include copper cladding and ground-face concrete block." It is a lovely building (and probably cost a pretty penny) but is surrounded by a tall chain-link fence topped with three strands of barbed wire, behind which is a tall hedge of conifers. The only access is via a locked gate, and the property is patrolled by a large and aggressive German Shepherd. The website has been "under construction" since I first viewed it four years ago, and a call to Talvan yielded only, "I am not comfortable with being interviewed."

The distillery's only product is *tzuika*, the Romanian name for plum brandy. It's sold as Mili Bit and can be found in about twenty Oregon liquor stores.

STEIN

A frequently cited reason for not making vodka from scratch is the cost of grain. One way to beat this is to grow it yourself, and that's exactly what's being done at Stein Distillery (DSP-OR-15023) in Joseph. Started in 2009 by Dan Stein (who does the distilling) and his son Austin (who handles the business side of things), the distillery sits on the family's 150-acre farm, planted with wheat and rye (corn is purchased from local farmers). Stein's Holstein still is equipped with two different columns, a short one for making whiskey and rum, and a tall one for neutral spirit. The neutral spirit is used as the base spirit for liqueurs as well as for vodka.[112]

Stein distills three different whiskeys, a bourbon, a rye and a wheat (this last one is not currently bottled on its own but is included in an all-straight whiskey blend). Stein is one of the few (possibly only) Oregon distilleries committed to a long-term aging program for its whiskey. Five-year-old versions of the bourbon and rye were released in 2015; the rye is a contender for best whiskey distilled in Oregon. The Steins originally planned to offer ten-year-old versions but may opt for eight-year-old instead. Being located in the "high desert" of eastern Oregon, the whiskey barrels experience a

Dan Stein of Stein Distillery. *Photo by the author.*

significant amount of evaporation loss (known in the industry as "angel's share"), so in 2016, the Steins began constructing a new wing where barrels can be stored and humidity levels better controlled.

The Stein vodka is made entirely from rye, the aroma of which is detectable to those with a keen sense of smell. At thirty-two dollars, it's pricey, but it's one of the few vodkas made entirely within the state.

Stein makes three rums, all from brown sugar. One of the dark rums is aged in ex-bourbon barrels.

The distillery also offers a line of liqueurs (which it calls cordials). An unusual one is the rhubarb, which is slightly sweet with a piquant character.

The town of Joseph is remote, so to give their products a little more visibility, the Steins opened a tasting room in Beaverton in 2015.

STONE BARN BRANDYWORKS

Sebastian and Erika Degens started Stone Barn Brandyworks (DSP-OR-15025) at the end of 2009. Located in a small industrial park in southeast Portland, the cinderblock building does not conform to what I would think of as a "stone barn," but the products made within are definitely the real article. All the raw materials are sourced from Oregon and fermented and distilled at the distillery. It's a pretty small operation, but it offers an extensive product line, with two whiskeys (rye and oat), two aged brandies (quince-pear and plum), two grappas (Malbec and Pinot Noir) and eight liqueurs, including a rhubarb (as far as I know only Stone Barn and Stein make this). Their apricot liqueur is very nice but is what I'd call semisweet and a little sour; otherwise, I'd recommend it for the cocktail described at the end of the Ransom section.

Rhubarb Daisy

2 ounces gin
1 ounce rhubarb liqueur
1 tablespoon lemon juice
½ tablespoon lime juice
1 ounce simple syrup
1 dash orange bitters
1 splash club soda

Shake all ingredients, except soda, with ice; strain into ice-filled cocktail glass. Top with club soda, and garnish with a lemon wedge.

11

HARD TIMES

If this chapter had a subtitle, it would be "A Case Study in Craft Distilling." The trials and tribulations of Hard Times Distillery in Monroe are admittedly atypical, but do serve as examples of the challenges that face those starting a distillery. The story is a cautionary tale for those considering such an enterprise.

Dudley Clark, a native of New Orleans, arrived in Oregon in 2004, settling in Junction City. Not long after, he met a local woman, with whom he started a family. Career-wise, he was engaged in a variety of activities, one of which was a show on a Eugene radio station. One of the other participants mentioned to Clark that he and a partner were planning to start a craft distillery; this piqued Clark's interest in the subject, and he spent time researching it.[113]

About a year later (during which the radio show ended), Clark received a call from the other individual. His prospective partner had backed out of the plan; would Clark be interested? He was, and Clark and his new partner (who shall remain unidentified, per both Clark and the ex-partner's request) began the process of starting a distillery.

Hard Times Distillery, LLC (DSP-OR-15026) was incorporated in January 2009, but it would be over a year before it produced any spirits. The first task was to find a location. Clark preferred Junction City, his partner Eugene, but they finally rented a former feed store in Monroe, mostly because the price was right. The partners applied for and received a loan via the Small Business Administration, receiving $20,000 (a lower amount than what they'd hoped and which had to be paid back in two $10,000 payments).

Over the course of a year, Clark and his partner obtained all the necessary licenses and permits from federal, state and municipal governments, as well as ordered the equipment needed for the operation. Their still was a custom unit; the pot was fabricated from a stainless steel fifty-five-gallon drum, which probably cost only a few hundred dollars, but the reflux column was ordered from the Amphora Society in Seattle and cost $3,000.

Whether by agreement or progression, Clark focused on the creative side of the enterprise while his partner was responsible for the business side. This latter responsibility included paying federal and state taxes and license fees and ensuring that all recording and reporting was in compliance with requirements. Clark's partner was also responsible for marketing and sales (this in addition to continuing a forty-hour-per-week job).

The distillery's official opening was on Sunday, May 16, 2010. The partners hired a bluegrass band and provided food and beverages. About fifty people attended.

The partners had originally planned to produce whiskey and vodka, both from rye. The equipment required for fermenting rye (a difficult grain to process, due to a tendency to clump during fermentation) was cost prohibitive, and Clark turned to the perennial favorite of those distilling on a budget: sugar. Sugar Momma vodka was released in mid-2010 for fifteen dollars per bottle. Although distilled to neutrality before cut to eighty proof, it had a slight but distinct rum nose (I suspect there was some molasses in with the sugar) and was exceptionally smooth. It was perfect for the sweeter types of vodka-based cocktails; I believe I made the best ever Harvey Wallbangers with it.

The next product was Green Geisha, wasabi-infused vodka, made from purchased neutral spirit and wasabi grown in Oregon. Restraint was exercised with the wasabi, and the flavor was in fact fairly subtle, though strong enough to show in a Bloody Mary.

Unfortunately, neither of these led to commercial success. Clark's partner did not have the time or the experience to excel at marketing and sales, and revenue lagged well behind expenses. The expenses included rent on the building, materials, electricity, state and federal fees and taxes and, of course, repayment of the loan. Clark's partner repeatedly expressed concern about operating in the red; Clark, an optimist by nature, kept hoping that things would turn around and revenues would eventually exceed expenses.

The year 2012 did start auspiciously. The distillery opened a tasting room in February, and Clark had a number of new products in the pipeline. In May, Sweet Baby Moonshine was introduced (of course, it's not really

The column still at Hard Times. *Photo by the author.*

moonshine because it was legally produced). Made from 50 percent oats, 45 percent barley and 5 percent cane sugar and bottled unaged, it drinks well on the rocks on a warm summer afternoon. The product sold reasonably well and remains in the distillery's lineup.

At the end of the year, things went sideways. Not only was the distillery behind on tax payments to the state and federal governments, but accounting and reporting were not in compliance with federal requirements. The amount of money owed, inflated by noncompliance fines, was of such magnitude that recovery seemed a dim prospect. Clark's partner no longer wanted to continue with the operation. "It was extremely stressful," he told me, "and I couldn't continue."

On December 20, 2012, Clark emailed an announcement to the Hard Times mailing list, stating that "I am being forced to close by circumstances too complicated and unpleasant to relate." He suggested those wishing to make final purchases visit the distillery the following weekend, as the distillery would be closing after that. He ended the email with: "I refuse to give up without a fight. I believe HT has a great deal of value, and lots more potential to delight and surprise. To that end, I hope soon to be in talks with interested parties in the hope of re-opening in 2013."

The "interested parties" were loyal customers who were willing to provide financial assistance, and on February 19, Clark announced that Hard Times would reopen on March 1. His partner, who by this time had left the company, was still personally responsible for the $4,000 owed to the OLCC (being the agent-of-record) and had to take out a personal loan to pay this. Clark was left with the majority of the debt, as well as being responsible for payment of noncompliance fines, but he negotiated a deferral of these.

Clark discontinued Sugar Momma vodka, replacing it with Blue Collar vodka, which is, I believe, made with purchased neutral spirit. Late in the year, Hard Times introduced its first liqueur, Appleshine, which added fresh apple cider, along with ginger, raisins and spices, to Sweet Baby Moonshine.

In May 2014, Hard Times began distilling malt whiskey and putting it into barrels. On June 1, the distillery opened a tasting room in downtown Eugene, located in the Whiteaker district. Yet another new activity for the distillery was hosting fee-paying guest distillers, individuals who made spirits of their own using Hard Times's equipment and under the auspices of the Hard Times licenses.

At the end of 2014, the malt whiskey was bottled as Eleventh Hour Whiskey. This was followed by Blue Collar Whiskey, unaged corn spirits that Clark purchased and then aged in barrels of Oregon oak.

The tasting room in Eugene had to relocate to Valley River Center mall, its previous dwelling place having been condemned. Unfortunately, it resided at the mall for only four months or so; it was a successful venue (Clark reported several "$3,000 days"), but the mall manager (a devout member of the LDS church) complained to the OLCC. Clark felt closure was the most expeditious course.

In 2015, Clark organized the first Hard Times Distillery Expo. Scheduled for August 15 and held at the Hult Center in Eugene, two dozen Oregon distilleries signed on for booths to showcase their wares. Three weeks prior to the event, Clark's youngest son was killed in a traffic accident; Clark went into seclusion and did not attend the expo. By this time, he'd moved

Dudley Clark, 2013. *Photo by the author.*

to Monroe, where he lived alone, his domestic partnership having ended some time earlier.

Eventually, Clark resumed active involvement with the distillery. He'd found a new partner, a "silent" one who does not really participate in distillery operations and is, essentially, an investor. Clark has also contracted with a number of professionals (CPA, attorney, et cetera) to ensure that taxes and fees are paid and the bookkeeping is done in compliance with federal requirements. He's also acquired a sales manager, and his eldest daughter (from a previous marriage) came on board in 2016 to handle restaurant and bar sales.

The current lineup includes Eleventh Hour Malt Whiskey, Blue Collar Whiskey, Blue Collar Vodka, Sweet Baby Moonshine and Appleshine (the

Green Geisha vodka is temporarily out of production, although as of this writing—September 21, 2016—www.oregonliquorsearch.com shows about thirty-nine bottles on liquor store shelves around the state).

In the course of interviewing Dudley Clark, it became clear that this is someone who prefers to talk about the future rather than the past. He's excited about his recent acquisition of two more stills, a Portuguese-made pot still of 165-gallon capacity and an Arnold Holstein still of 85-gallon capacity. He's got two rye whiskeys in the pipeline; the first, made for him by Blue Flame Distillery in Prosser, Washington, is labeled Blind Faith and will be released in late 2016, to be followed by Fool Proof, which was distilled at Hard Times from Oregon-grown rye. He's planning to move the distillery to Corvallis and in mid-2016 was scouting locations (Clark himself now resides there). He also expects to soon settle the $18,000 debt he has with the federal government and is planning another tasting room, this one at the Lancaster Mall in Salem.

Perhaps most encouraging of all is that Clark is continuing with the Hard Times Distillery Expo, with the second one held on August 6, 2016, again at the Hult Center in Eugene (future expos will probably be later in the year so as not be so close in time to the McMenamins-sponsored Oregon Distillers Festival held at Edgefield in July).

We wish him the best of luck.

Snidely's Whiplash

1½ ounces Sweet Baby Moonshine
1 ounce orange-lime-ginger syrup (recipe follows)
½ ounce lemon juice
1 teaspoon honey
2 ounces cold-brew tea
club soda to taste

Shake all ingredients with ice; strain into highball glass. Add one large ice cube, top with club soda and garnish with lemon or lime twist.

Orange-Lime-Ginger Syrup

1 cup sugar
½ cup water
2 tablespoons chopped fresh ginger

2 teaspoons orange rind
½ teaspoon lime juice

Cook all ingredients in a small saucepan over low heat until sugar dissolves. Bring to a boil; reduce heat, and simmer for 1 minute.

Remove from heat; let stand 15 minutes. Remove and discard ginger and orange rind. Cool syrup; chill 1 hour or up to 3 days.

Note: Remove rind from an orange using a vegetable peeler or paring knife. Avoid the bitter white pith as much as possible.

12

A HUNDRED SPLENDID SUNS

The pace of distillery creation has increased dramatically since 2010, both nationally and in Oregon. Here in the Beaver State, where only twenty-six DSP licenses were assigned from 1984 through mid-2009 (up through Hard Times), at least thirty-six have been assigned in the seven years since then (it's hard to get the exact number because the IRS TTB divulges DSP numbers only indirectly, as part of a distillery's information on a Certificate of Label Approval request).

Oregon's current count of operating (or soon to be operating) distilleries is somewhere between sixty-two and seventy-five (the latter figure being the number of current operating licenses granted by the TTB). We haven't reached one hundred, and whether we will is an open question. Some, including myself, believe we will; others believe attrition will prevent it.

And of those distilleries currently operating, not all deserve to be called "splendid." Those that don't are the ones that simply bring in spirits from outside the state, bottle them and put "Produced in Oregon" on the label. The worst offenders are those who claim to be distilling but in fact are not (more on this later).

A question I'm frequently asked is why are so many distilleries being opened, both nationally and in Oregon. As for the national trend, I think it's part of a larger phenomenon that includes a similar proliferation of wineries and craft breweries and that, in turn, is part of an even larger trend of consumers wanting both more choices and better choices. Fifty years ago, we drank Folgers and Maxwell House, bland lagers from Budweiser and Miller and blended whiskey from Seagram's, and if we drank wine at all, it was something from Italian Swiss Colony. Since then we've evolved to expect a diversity of food and drink options, and the entrepreneurial spirit that's always characterized Americans meant many realized they could profit by meeting this demand.

The pioneering winemakers, brewers and distillers were those members of the boomer generation who took "do your own thing" literally, as opposed to the majority who might have quoted that phrase in their youth but ultimately spent their careers in salaried positions. These last were for the most part successful, but often felt unfulfilled and, particularly in recent years, were victims of layoffs by their employers, companies to which they'd given years of loyal service. Their children, observing this, adopted a "follow your passion" ethic, and it's not surprising that many of the latest wave of breweries, distilleries and wineries are being started by members of Generation Y and late Generation X.

The second part of the question—whether Oregon is exceptionally prolific in creating distilleries—can be answered by examining some data.

First, in terms of per-capita number of distilleries, Oregon ranks fourth:

Distilleries per 100,000[114]

Vermont	4.15
Washington	2.09
Montana	1.94
Oregon	**1.86**
Colorado	1.65

It does better with craft breweries:

Craft breweries per 100,000[115]

Vermont	9.4
Oregon	**7.7**
Colorado	7.3
Montana	6.5
Washington	5.9

And even better with wineries:

Wineries per 100,000[116]

Oregon   **17.49**
California   10.44
Washington   10.43
Vermont   4.79
Idaho   2.90

So, clearly, there is something about Oregon that fosters a willingness to get into alcoholic beverage production. What would that be?

One factor is demand, of course. Oregon ranks eleventh in per-capita consumption of alcohol, but perhaps it's more enlightening to define the cultural context of alcohol in the state. For that, we have a survey done in 2014 by Chris Kolmar, who used ten different metrics (such as per-capita consumption and days per week alcohol is sold) and found that Oregon is the "booziest" state in the United States, followed by Colorado, Alaska, Montana, Vermont, Wisconsin and Washington.[117]

So why are Oregonians so receptive to alcohol production and consumption? There are a couple of studies that have tried to associate personality types with regions, and these might provide some insight. One, published by the American Psychological Association, defined three broad personality types. On "Friendly and Conventional," Oregon scored low (with Washington slightly higher and Vermont slightly lower), on "Relaxed and Creative," Oregon scores very high (Washington slightly lower and Vermont just above average) and on "Temperamental and Uninhibited," Oregon is just below average (Washington slightly lower and Vermont scores high).[118] Another study, by the "16 Personalities" group, finds that Oregon scores high in the "Explorer/Adventurer" category (as does Vermont, with Washington slightly lower). The study goes on to state, "Vermont and Oregon…have reputations for attracting freethinkers and harboring those with alternative lifestyles."[119] Interestingly, Oregon, Washington and Vermont all score slightly lower in the "Explorer/Entrepreneur" category, which suggests that the motive to do something new is more important than the motive to make money.

Religion is another factor. Being from the South, I am well aware that conservative denominations, such as Baptists, incorporate proscription of alcohol into their dogma. According to a 2016 Pew Research study, Oregon

McMenamins Edgefield hosts the Oregon Distillers Festival in Troutdale. *Photo by the author (July 2016).*

is the eleventh-lowest state where adults declare themselves to be "highly religious" (Vermont is third lowest and Washington sixth).[120] Portland is even less religious, with a Gallup poll from early 2016 finding the city tied with San Francisco and Seattle as having the lowest percentage of people claiming a religious affiliation.[121]

Yet another reason for the distillery boom is Oregon's status as a "foodie" state. We Oregonians appreciate excellence in the production and preparation of what we eat and drink, including beer, wine and spirits. There are also lots of "locavores," people who prefer food and beverages produced within the state, and who are willing to make the extra effort to purchase a local product.

The year 2007 saw the formation of the Oregon Distiller's Guild. The first of its kind in the nation, the guild is a nonprofit corporation intended to promote the common interests of Oregon's licensed distilleries. Started with a $5,000 grant from the Portland Development Commission, some of the originally stated goals were:

- develop tools and strategies that will enable members to improve efficiencies and reduce operating costs
- bulk purchasing of supplies
- work with regulatory bodies to improve business conditions.[122]

It's not clear to an outsider how many of these goals have actually been achieved. One owner of a member distillery told me that there hasn't been a lot of information exchange, saying, "Many of the members are pretty secretive." During a recent conversation with one of the four board members I was told that "communications are lax." There is one live meeting per year (usually pretty well attended), with nine or ten teleconference meetings; these last are lightly attended.

Most members I've interviewed do agree that the organization has been successful in its lobbying efforts, and it can take credit for proposing many of the statutory changes enacted since 2008.

The annual membership fee is $350. In mid-2008, there were sixteen members; by mid-2016, this had grown to thirty-two, a little less than half the number of operating distilleries in the state.

The guild operates a members-only online forum in conjunction with its website, and some equipment resales have been facilitated by this feature. Again, I was told by a board member that activity on the forum is "light."

The guild is planning some changes to improve its communications and recruitment efforts. These include:

- Increasing the board size to at least five, possibly seven.
- Better forum software for the guild website.
- Additional membership categories, such as "Enthusiast."

The organization's biggest undertaking is its annual Toast event. Held in downtown Portland in February, this showcases distillers from both Oregon and Washington, and food is provided by several local restaurants.

Apart from the guild-sponsored Toast, there are a couple other events of note. McMenamins sponsors the Oregon Distillers Festival, which is held in late July at its Edgefield venue in Troutdale. This event usually hosts about twenty-five distilleries and attracts several hundred visitors. Hard Times Distillery sponsors the Hard Times Distillery Expo, which features twenty to twenty-four distilleries and producers of specialty fermented beverages. Hosted at the Hult Center in Eugene, in 2015 and 2016 it was held in mid-August, but from 2017 onward, it will probably be held a little later in the year.

The OLCC, which Steve McCarthy described as being indifferent to his efforts during the 1980s and '90s, began to take more notice of the Oregon distilling movement during the first decade of the twenty-first century and by 2008 was engaged in internal discussions about how best to support the industry. The agency supported the legislation that year that allowed tasting rooms and sales to visitors. In February 2009, an article appeared on the OLCC blog entitled "Want to Start Your Own Craft Distillery?" The article is generally encouraging and directs the reader to the OLCC homepage. Currently, there are no direct links from that page to any helpful information, but by following the link to the Liquor Stores and Products page, you'll find a link to Starting Your Own Craft Distillery. This page describes the general process of starting a distillery and provides links to other relevant webpages.

Beginning in 2011, the OLCC began tracking and reporting the "Oregon Products" percentage of overall spirits sales. In that year, $53.8 million of "Oregon Products" were sold, or about 12 percent of the total. By 2015, the dollar amount had risen to $69.3 million. It should be understood, however, that "Oregon Product" is anything sold by an Oregon company. In fact, looking at the sales ordered listing of 750-milliliter bottles sold in 2015, it's not until you get to item no. 45 that you find a spirit made entirely within Oregon.

In 2012, Rob Patridge became chair of the Oregon Liquor Control Commission, and in 2013, Steve Marks became the agency's executive director. Both Patridge and Marks are advocates for Oregon businesses and have continued the agency's efforts to support Oregon distillers. The OLCC has coordinated with the Oregon Distillers Guild to work out the details of bills submitted by state legislators wishing to support the state's distilling industry.[123]

One significant change in the statutes, passed in 2015, allows direct bulk sales of spirits from one Oregon distiller to another. Both in this chapter and in chapter 10 are there vodka and gin producers reported as buying their base spirit from out-of-state distillers; with this change in the law, it is hoped that some enterprising party in the state will start producing neutral spirits that can be sold at a competitive price, allowing the vodka and gin producers to market "all Oregon" products (I'd do it if I thought a bank would loan me the money—we're talking eight figures here). An initiative that did not make it through the legislative process in 2015 was a proposal to create a state distillery board modeled on the Oregon Wine Board. Hopefully some future session of the legislature will correct this oversight.

As stated at the beginning of the chapter, over thirty-five distilleries have opened since mid-2009. Space considerations prevent lengthy descriptions of each of these, but hopefully the following summaries will suffice.

Oregon Spirit Distillers (DSP-OR-15028) was started in 2009 by Brad Irwin. Located in Bend, the distillery is best known for its C.W. Irwin bourbon and is the largest distiller of bourbon in Oregon. At forty dollars it's a bit pricey for three-year-old bourbon, but it's probably the best one made entirely within the state. According to the OLCC, 4,807 bottles were sold between August 1, 2015, and August 1, 2016. Of greater interest from a historical perspective is the Ottis Webber wheat whiskey. The first modern wheat whiskey made in Oregon, it recalls the wheat whiskeys made in the state during the nineteenth century and, like the bourbon, is three years old and forty dollars per bottle. The distillery also produces vodka, Genever-style gin, spiced rum and absinthe. Notably, the lead distiller, Molly Troupe, is not only one of the state's only female distillers but also probably the only Oregon distiller with a degree in the subject, having received a master's of science in brewing and distilling from Heriot-Watt University (Edinburgh, Scotland) in 2013.

Immortal Spirits (DSP-OR-15029) was founded by Jesse Gallagher and Rico Carini, who were originally considering opening a microbrewery but decided to get into distilling after visiting a distillery in Portland. The distillery, located on the south side of Medford, is notable for its large-capacity still (eight hundred gallons) fabricated from a stainless steel storage tank (there is also a smaller-capacity still for specialty spirits). The

Owner Brad Irwin and distiller Molly Troupe of Oregon Spirit Distillery. *Photo by the author.*

partners produce three varieties of whiskey (one is unaged), vodka (from purchased neutral spirit), rum, gin, absinthe, pear eau de vie, Nocino (walnut liqueur) and a three-year-old blackberry brandy (I'm pretty sure this is a unique offering). In late 2015, Immortal Spirits opened a tasting room in downtown Medford.

Ye Ol' Grog Distillery (DSP-OR-15032) is the creation of four engineers: Marcus Albin, Lloyd Williams, Greg Scott and Ken McFarland. The St. Helens distillery makes vodka, the neutral spirit for which is either

Jesse Gallagher of Immortal Spirits. *Photo by the author.*

purchased or distilled by YOGD itself from fermented sugar solution, depending on the current price of commodity neutral spirit. When using purchased spirit, they redistill it making very aggressive cuts and end up with about 80 percent of the original volume. Their still is a sophisticated custom unit that they designed themselves. YOGD's products are several types of vodka (sold under the St. Helens brand), including one, M-91, bottled at

170 proof (that's 85 percent ABV!). The lineup also includes two variants of what's called "grog." These are really just flavored vodkas (there is no legal definition for "grog"—the stuff served to British seamen until 1970 was simply watered-down rum) and are sold as "Dutch Harbor Breeze" and "Good Morning Glory." "Basically what we do is make fun, unpretentious alcohol," Lloyd Williams told me. In the case of the M-91 vodka, we're talking *highly concentrated* fun.

Big Bottom (DSP-OR-15033) was founded by Ted Pappas in 2010 and is located in an industrial park in Hillsboro. Initially, Pappas was simply bringing in barreled whiskey from eastern distillers and bottling it. Pappas eventually began "finishing" the whiskey in the manner of some Scottish malt distillers, giving it additional time in barrels that previously held some type of wine (at Big Bottom, these were ex-port, Cabernet and Zinfandel barrels).

I spoke with Pappas in late 2010 and asked him about future plans. He told me he hoped to acquire a still and begin distilling his own product. This came to pass in 2012, when Big Bottom purchased a one-hundred-gallon still and hired Travis Shoney to operate it. Shoney was recently arrived from Utah, where he'd worked at High West, a Utah company known for its creative blends of whiskeys acquired from MGP and elsewhere and which was doing some distilling of its own. Shoney's first creation was Barlow whiskey, a blend of straight whiskeys with "light" whiskey. Light whiskey is the American variant of grain whiskey, which is the distilled-at-high-proof whiskey blended with malt whiskeys in Scotland to produce "blended" Scotch (the kind most people drink). The light whiskey purchased by Big Bottom was distilled at MGP, made for Diageo, who use it in the export version of Seagram's Seven, which, unlike the American version, has to be 100 percent whiskey. Apparently MGP has lots of old stocks of light whiskey; High West recently purchased one hundred barrels of fourteen-year-old light whiskey from MGP.

More recently, Big Bottom has distilled gin (two different proof levels), as well as apple and pear brandy. About half the brandy was barreled, with the other half bottled unaged. The unaged apple brandy is the first of its type bottled in Oregon since Eve Atkins distillery shut down in 1997.

Pappas and Shoney have ambitious plans and are negotiating with Vendome for a larger still.

4 Spirits Distillery (DSP-OR-15037) was started by Dawson Officer in 2010. Located in the old blockhouse building in what was Camp Adair Air Force Base, the first products were bourbon and vodka. The bourbon comes from Indiana and is given some extra barrel time at 4 Spirits. The vodka is made from purchased neutral spirit, redistilled and filtered at 4 Spirits. The vodka is sold under the 4 Spirits name, but also originally appeared as Slaptail, with the label using Oregon State colors, and Webfoot, with the label using University of Oregon colors (since then more variations have appeared, using names and colors of other Pacific Northwest universities). Light rum and spiced rum, both made from a mix of sugar and molasses, appeared in 2014, with dark rum in 2015 and habanero rum in 2016. 4 Spirits has been a successful operation and has outgrown its current facility. A new distillery is being built (not yet complete in August 2016) on the south side of Corvallis, next door to the recently completed Block 15 brewery. At 6,800 square feet, it will accommodate a bigger still and considerably more barrel storage.

Dogwood Distilling (DSP-OR-15039) was started by Matt Hottenroth and Jasin Hope in 2011. The Forest Grove distillery aims to produce spirits priced low enough to be well brands at Oregon bars. The distillery purchases corn-based neutral spirit that Hottenroth redistills in a still of his own design and construction. Dogwood currently offers DL Franklin vodka (sixteen dollars) and "Union" gin (twenty-two dollars), along with the pricier Haint absinthe (twenty-nine dollars for a 375-milliliter bottle).

Elixir (DSP-OR-15041) is located in Eugene and was founded by two Italian brothers, Andrea and Mario Loreto. Using purchased organically produced neutral grain spirit, the brothers produce two liqueurs: Calisaya, a traditional Italian liqueur made from a plant that originated in South America; and Iris, made from iris root. I've tried them both, and I prefer the Calisaya, the Iris being a little tart.

Vivacity Spirits (DSP-OR-15046), located just north of Corvallis, is one of only five distilleries in the United States owned by a woman. Caitlin Prueitt, along with her spouse, Chris Neumann, and some hired help, produce vodka, two types of gin, rum and a coffee liqueur. The vodka and gin originate as purchased neutral spirit, but Prueitt redistills it to provide consistency of aroma and flavor, her still imparting its own character. Her 130-gallon still is notable because it is one of only three in the state made by Vendome, the firm that supplied House Spirits with its large-capacity still (in fact, I didn't know Vendome made stills this small until I saw the one at Vivacity).

Bull Run (DSP-OR-15049) was started by Lee Medoff in 2012 after he left House Spirits. Partnering with Patrick Bernards, Medoff wanted to focus on whiskey and after acquiring a site in northwest Portland, purchased two eight-hundred-gallon stills and began producing and barreling malt whiskey, along with smaller quantities of rye whiskey. The first bottlings of these will be released in October 2016. In the meantime, Bull Run has been purchasing bourbon and light whiskey from distillers in Indiana, Kentucky and Tennessee and selling these under the Temperance Trader label. Some of the bourbon has been aged in ex-vermouth barrels and sold as Temperance Trader Chinato. The Temperance Trader label is being discontinued, but these whiskeys will continue to be sold under the Bull Run name. Medoff is planning to re-barrel ("finish") some of the bourbon in barrels previously used to age Pinot Noir.

Medoff brought Medoyeff vodka with him from House Spirits; in 2015, a barrel-aged version, Starka, was introduced.

Bull Run had also been producing light rum, known as Pacific Rum, made from Hawaiian molasses. This was recently discontinued, but a barrel-aged version will be released in late 2016.

Patrick Bernards, who reportedly felt the IRS TTB rules regulating whiskey production were too restrictive, left Bull Run in mid-2016 to pursue another project.

Industrial Row Distillery (DSP-OR-15053) is owned and operated by Nelson D'Amour. The Portland distillery produces one product, Dystopia Vodka, but is one of the few grain-to-bottle vodka producers in the state.

Barrel storage at Bull Run distillery. *Photo by the author.*

D'Amour purchases wheat and rye from Bob's Red Mill, ferments it, distills it in a large copper column still, blends and bottles it. He emphatically states that his spirit requires no filtering (visit the dystopiavodka.com website for an entertaining list of substances used to filter vodka).

Cannon Beach Distillery (DSP-OR-20001) was started by Mike Seiberg in 2011. Seiberg distills all of his products in a one-hundred-gallon Vendome still. Most of his spirits are made from some variant of sugar cane byproduct (cane juice or molasses). He makes two types of rum, the first being Donlon Shanks, a traditional type made from molasses, and Doryman's, a lighter type made in the style of Brazilian cachaça and made from cane juice. The same fermented cane juice is distilled to neutrality and then used to make three different gins, one of which, the Pharmacist, is an Old Tom gin but, unlike most gins in that category, spends no time in a barrel. A more recent product is Il Keyote, which is made from fermented agave juice. No, it's not tequila (it can't be legally called that) and has a hint of sweetness that most tequila lacks, but it works in a margarita (perhaps with a little less triple sec than usual). In August 2016, Seiberg released Eventide, his first whiskey, which sold out in two days.

Sinister Distilling Company (DSP-OR-20004) of Albany is an outgrowth of Deluxe Brewing Company, both owned by Eric Howard. His still, a traditional copper still from the Alembic Still Company of Portugal, is fairly small (forty-gallon capacity), and it requires four passes through this still to make the base spirit for his gin, Howard's Hopped Up Gin. The spirit is well short of neutrality, but that gives it the malty overtones associated with a traditional Genever. Howard has some whiskey he's had in ex-wine barrels since mid-2015; bottling and release date are still unknown. In the autumn of 2016, he's planning to make grappa from pomace obtained from Emerson Vineyards.

Cascade Alchemy (DSP-OR-20004) of Bend was started by Tyler Fradet and Joe Hale in 2012. Later joined by Joe's brother James, their small, locally fabricated still could not make neutral spirit (maxing out around 88 percent ABV), so to make their vodka, they use purchased neutral spirit. Their own still is used for gin (they use the same local *Juniperus occidentalis* berries as Bendistillery) and for their unaged barley whiskey (Barleyshine). They have a bourbon in the product lineup, but it's purchased unaged from an out-of-state distiller (probably MGP) and then aged, cut and bottled at Cascade's facility in Bend. Two flavored vodkas (Chai Tea and Hot Pepper) and an apple liqueur complete the product lineup.

Camp 1805 (DSP-OR-20007) in Hood River was opened in 2014 by partners Roy Slayton and Chris Taylor. The name references the probability that Lewis and Clark would have camped in the vicinity on their way to the

Pacific. The Camp 1805 vodka (Mt. Hood Vodka) is made from purchased neutral spirit, filtered at Camp 1805, cut with local water and bottled. Camp 1805 has a lovely hand-hammered copper still that it uses for making its whiskey (sold unaged as Endurance White Whiskey) and white rum (Backbone).

Roy Slayton, co-owner of Camp 1805 Distillery. *Photo by the author.*

Rolling River (DSP-OR-20008) is a family affair, located in Portland and founded by Rick Rickard. Wife Joan and son Tim do the distilling, with daughter Elizabeth handling marketing. Although Rolling River purchases neutral spirit, it redistills in its own column still and uses the output as the basis for its vodka, gin and aquavit. It also has a 120-gallon pot still that it uses for the gin and aquavit second distillation and for making whiskey, the unaged version of which was released in mid-2016.

Spiritopia (DSP-OR-20011), located north of Corvallis in the same small industrial park as Vivacity, was started by chemist Chris Beatty, who originally intended to make a spirit from Oregon Ryegrass. The TTB didn't have a classification for spirits made from grass, so that's on hold until the red tape gets unwound. Beatty is concentrating on liqueurs in the meantime and in 2015 changed the name from Oregon Ryegrass Spirits to the current one. The first liqueur was apple, followed by ginger and pomegranate. Beatty distills the base spirit for these and in early 2016 decided that two barrels of the apple brandy were good enough to bottle on their own. I've sampled the product, aged in charred oak barrels of thirty-gallon capacity, and can attest to the "bourbon character" claimed for it.

Stillwagon Distillery (DSP-OR-20012) is located south of Charleston, a coastal town west of Coos Bay. Rick Stillwagon is a rum specialist and distills all of his products in his own custom still. In addition to traditional white and gold rums, he produces several spiced and flavored varieties, as well as vodka made from molasses. This last is exceptionally smooth and a worthy successor to the now-defunct Sugar Momma from Hard Times. Stillwagon also makes his own extracts for his infusions.

Perhaps the most significant creation from Stillwagon will not be a distilled spirit but rather a system for recycling the carbon dioxide generated during the fermentation process, the goal being to achieve a zero-carbon footprint. While showing me a PowerPoint presentation of the system, Stillwagon said, "It's just a matter of time before there's a carbon tax, and when that happens, every brewery, winery and distillery in the United States is going to need something like this."

"And with you having this patented and ready to go," I replied, "you're going to become a rich man."

"Well, yes, but that's not why I'm doing this. The goal is to do something about carbon emissions."

And, yes, I believe him. Rick Stillwagon is the archetypical Oregon artisan, committed not just to his craft but also to the ideals of sustainability and environmental harmony. He's got my support, and

Rick Stillwagon. *Photo by the author.*

when I finish my last bottle of Sugar Momma vodka, I'll be getting a bottle of his Persian Reed.

DSP-OR-20014 was assigned to North Coast Distilling of Astoria. Founded by Lawrence Cary in 2013, the distillery was sued by a California brewery, North Coast Brewing. Cary changed the name to Pilot House Spirits. The ink was barely dry on the paperwork when they received a cease-and-desist order from House Spirits of Portland, which subsequently sued when Cary did not comply. The lawsuit was settled when the Astoria distillery changed its name to **Pilot House Distilling**.

Pilot House is equipped with a still (capacity unknown), which is probably used for redistillation of neutral spirit as part of the vodka and gin production process. The Pilot House rum is almost certainly distilled in this still as well. The AO Whiskey is described as "American light whiskey," which means it's sourced from a midwestern distillery, probably MGP (but not necessarily; there are a few other distilleries with stocks of light whiskey).

Crescendo (DSP-OR-20015) is a Eugene company that uses purchased organic neutral spirit to produce three liqueurs. These are limoncello, limecello and arancello (orange). All three are good, but the arancello is a standout.

Tualatin Valley Distilling (DSP-OR-20016) was founded by Corey Bowers and Jason O'Donnell. Currently operating out of leased space at Big Bottom in Hillsboro, the partners redistill purchased neutral spirit and use the output as a base spirit for their absinthe and their Usquebaugh-flavored vodka. Notable are their whiskeys, which they make in a small (twenty-six-gallon) pot still. These are Oregon Single Malt made from malted barley and 50/50 whiskey, which is half malted barley and half rye. This is, as far as I know, a unique mashbill, and the resulting whiskey has an intriguing smokiness, despite the malt being unsmoked. The aging time is pretty short (a little over six months) and the barrels rather small (five to six gallons), but I have to admit it's not bad whiskey. Here's hoping that Bowers and O'Donnell are successful enough to not only get their own digs but also be able to age the whiskey longer and in bigger barrels.

Table Rock Distillery (DSP-OR-20022) is a tiny distillery in Eagle Point, a town about ten miles north of Medford. Owner Gary Thompson distills whiskey from peat-smoked malt imported from Scotland and then ages it for fourteen months in medium-toasted barrels of eight-gallon capacity. A small amount of gin is also produced; this is sold only at the distillery (visits by appointment only).

New Basin (DSP-OR-20023) is a five-way partnership (Rick Molitor, Ryan Boyle, Chris Tatro, Tom Norton Jr. and Greg Williams) and is located in Madras, a town of about 6,500 and located about forty miles north of Bend. The partners have the admirable goal of eventually producing "all Oregon" spirits, using locally grown grain and aging in barrels of Oregon oak. They acquired a large still on March 1, 2016, but it was not yet operational in July when I spoke to one of the partners at the Oregon

Distillers Festival at Edgefield. To get something to market, the company has purchased neutral spirits from out-of-state suppliers and used this for its vodka, gin and light whiskey, which they bottle and sell as eight-year-old Strong American Light Whiskey. The New Basin partner with whom I spoke was vague about their source for the light whiskey, but it's probable that it's MGP in Indiana, that being the only distillery in the United States producing light whiskey in any quantity.

At present (August 2016), New Basin is very much a work-in-progress.

Wild Roots (DSP-OR-20024) is another vodka infuser. The company taps into Bendistillery's source of neutral spirit and does its infusions there. Bottling is done at another facility in Hillsboro. Currently raspberry, marionberry and apple-cinnamon are offered.

Thomas and Sons Distillery (DSP-OR-20025) is a project of Matt Thomas, whose first company is Townshend Tea. The Portland distillery produces a unique line of liqueurs made from sweetened and fermented tea, using a custom continuous still that produces spirit at 60 percent. The low distillation proof makes for a distinctively flavored product (as in, you know it was made from tea). In 2015, the company introduced Bluebird Alpine Liqueur and in 2016 its version of Fernet, a traditional Italian liqueur.

Backdrop Distilling (DSP-OR-20026) in Bend was started in late 2014 by Mark Plants. Using a sixty-five-gallon German still, Plants redistills purchased neutral spirit to produce vodka, the only current product. Rum and gin are in the works.

III Spirits (DSP-OR-20028) was started in 2014 by Todd Kemp (a former brewer) and Alex Turner (a marine engineer). Located on a farm near Talent and housed in a 720-square-foot building constructed by the partners, the distillery has been producing malt-based whiskeys and released its first bottlings in mid-2016. Its first still was one the partners built themselves, but in mid-2016, they acquired a 185-gallon Hoga unit. Their first whiskeys were aged only a year in five- and ten-gallon barrels, but they've started buying larger barrels and hope to age for longer periods. They'll also be opening a tasting room in the autumn of 2016.

Davis Distributing Company (DSP-OR-20029) of Eugene has one product, Hardass Vodka, which it produces by redistilling purchased neutral spirits.

Martin Ryan Distilling (DSP-OR-20030) was started by Erik Martin and Ryan Csansky, whose earlier effort, Artisan Distilling, closed in 2010. The new company was devoted to one product, Aria gin, which they produced at Bull Run until 2015, when they acquired their own facility in northwest Portland. The partners use their own eight-hundred-gallon still to produce gin from purchased neutral spirit.

Marble Caves Distillery (DSP-OR-20031) of Cave Junction was started in 2015 by Roderick Warner, a recently retired chemistry and biology high school teacher from Eureka, California. It's a modest operation; his still is only ten-gallon capacity, and he's been turning out small quantities of apple and pear brandy and a slightly larger quantity of rum.

Cascadia Artisan Distillery (DSP-OR-20033) produces only one spirit, Vilya absinthe, but they do it extremely well. At wormwoodsociety. org, of 198 rated "traditional" absinthes sold around the world, Vilya is ranked ninth overall and is third on the list of those available in the United States. Owner/distiller Jazper Torres was originally making Vilya at Ridge Distillery in Montana but recently moved the operation to Cave Junction, where his family owned property. Torres lives in Bend and commutes to Cave Junction once a week to produce a batch; he's hoping to move the operation to Bend at some future date.

Wolf Spirits (DSP-OR-20035) of Eugene produces Bell Kurve vodka from winter wheat, using a still from Artisan Still Design.

Swallowtail Spirits (no DSP yet assigned) was one of the producers using the Hard Times facility and producing under the Hard Times DSP. It had been using purchased neutral spirits and cutting them with local well water, but the owners are currently building their own facility in Springfield, which will be equipped with its own still. Owner Kevin Barrett and distiller Matthew McLain plan to make a peated malt whiskey in the Islay style.

This is not a full list of distilleries started in the last seven years. There are a number of reasons why some were omitted, the most frequent one being that I had questions I wanted answered about those distilleries but was unable to contact the owners. There are probably also one or two distilleries that I simply missed.

13

SOME CLOSING THOUGHTS

When I started researching this book in 2012, I had a number of preconceptions that did not fully survive the process. Most of these concerned the use of spirits distilled elsewhere and bottled in Oregon (I've become more forgiving about this). Additionally, I developed some new beliefs based on knowledge acquired along the way. What follows are my current views on several subjects.

TRANSPARENCY

I've spoken with nearly every distillery owner in the state and met most of them. Almost without exception they are an honest lot, but, yes, there are exceptions. There are at least two who claim to be fermenting and distilling everything they sell but who, I'm certain, aren't distilling anything at all. No, I'm not going to say who they are (I'd want to get proof first); in fact, they're not even mentioned in the book (this does not mean that a distillery not mentioned in the book is one of those two; as stated at the end of chapter 12, unlisted distilleries are mostly those whose owners I was never able to contact).

Also worth mentioning are those who import whiskey distilled in another state and who don't reference this on the bottle's label. If you ask, they will admit they didn't distill it, but that doesn't count. The Code of Federal Regulations (Title 27/Chapter I/Subchapter A/Part 5/Section 36/subsection D) states:

State of distillation. Except in the case of "light whisky," "blended light whisky," "blended whisky," "a blend of straight whiskeys," or "spirit whisky," the State of distillation shall be shown on the label of any whisky produced in the United States if the whisky is not distilled in the State given in the address on the brand label.

So if you're bringing in bourbon or rye that was distilled in another state and not identifying that state on your label, then you are in violation of federal law. If you've gotten away with that so far, it's a matter of luck, and luck, my friend, has a way of running out.

"PRODUCED IN OREGON"

There is, unfortunately, no legal definition of this phrase, and that's bad news for those who'd like to extend their "buy local" ethic to spirits. Ideally, it could only be used for spirits whose raw material originated in Oregon and were fermented and distilled here. Such spirits are the exception rather than the rule, and only consumers who've spent a lot of time educating themselves are going to know the difference. There are those who believe—and I'm one of them—that they should not have to do that.

Among Oregon producers this is a contentious topic. I recently visited one who became quite defensive and called me a "purist" when I brought up the subject. I pointed out that a purist does not recognize the existence of "gray" areas; bringing in not fully aged whiskey and keeping it in the barrel until the Oregon producer deems it ready is not the same thing as bringing in fully mature whiskey and simply bottling it.

From the locavore's perspective, however, neither of these production paradigms is acceptable. I don't have to agree with the locavores to advocate for them, because it comes down to whether you believe in choice, and I most assuredly do (here's an analogous example: I believe wearing a helmet should be the motorcyclist's choice, but I will always wear one).

So how do we accommodate those who wish to apply a strict standard to "buying local"?

A MODEST PROPOSAL

The state of Washington drops the annual fee for distilling from $2,000 to $100 if the distiller uses at least 50 percent Washington-grown materials. I'm not in favor of that sort of standard because it unfairly penalizes the rum producers (reality check for the locavores: sugar cane does not grow in the Pacific Northwest). I'd suggest a certification standard for "Fermented and Distilled in Oregon." Certifying a product to that standard could be encouraged by the OLCC reducing its markup on it (the modest loss of revenue could be offset by any number of methods), and placing it on the label would let the consumer know it's more likely to have been locally produced than a spirit that lacks that.

OREGON PRODUCTION OF NEUTRAL SPIRITS

Nearly every producer in the state brings in neutral spirits purchased from non-Oregon distillers. Most neutral spirits are produced in the Midwest at huge distilleries that resemble oil refineries, and the economy of scale is such that the price of the product is quite low. Production on that scale within Oregon would not have been possible until 2015 because until then, it was not legal for one distillery in the state to sell directly to another.

With the statutory restrictions eliminated, would such an enterprise be practical here? I've been told that the Distiller's Guild looked into this and decided it would not be because it would cost $30 million to build a plant that could price its product competitively. I'm not sure I believe that, and I think it might be sufficient to simply approach the price of the Midwest producers. It's a subject that I believe warrants additional investigation, and I plan to do just that.

OREGON DISTILLERY BOARD

In chapter 12, I reported that in 2015, the Oregon legislature failed to approve a distillery board modeled on the Oregon Wine Board. This should be rectified as soon as possible. One change I would suggest: the OWB is composed entirely of winery owners; I think an ODB should include representation from the state's liquor store owners and a consumer advocate as well (I'm available, but only if there's income associated with the position).

PRIVATIZATION

In principle, I'm against state-operated liquor monopolies. I believe in the free market system, and I don't like the state to have the level of control that it has in Oregon. But principles, though they are wonderful things to have, don't always work well in the real world. Sure, kept inside, on the shelf next to your badminton trophies, they're bright and shiny, but take them outside and they quickly tarnish, turning a pukey green color.

That's how it is with privatization. The state of Washington is an educational case study; when the majority of the state's voters chose privatization, the state government retaliated by raising liquor taxes to the highest in the nation, an act so adversarial in nature that it should dispel anyone's belief that modern American governments are of the people, by the people and for the people.

Another result was to squeeze out smaller, independent liquor stores, ones that made an effort to stock spirits produced by Washington distillers. The effect on the state's craft distillers was devastating; I was told by a member of the OLCC that Washington distillers have been trying hard to get more of their products into Oregon liquor stores.

In fact, I have not met a single current Oregon distiller who favors privatization. So if it ever comes up for a vote here, I'm voting against it. You should, too.

TIME IN THE BARREL

Nearly all Oregon whiskeys are too young. One to two years is the norm, three years is unusual, four years is exceptional and five is positively ancient by Oregon standards. If Oregon whiskey makers want to create spirits that compare to what's coming out of Kentucky, six years is a minimum. Yes, I understand that it's a challenge to defer the return on investment. Consider getting investors. Worried about losing control of your company? Look into non-voting stock.

Oh, and ditch the tiny barrels. Fifty-three gallons is the standard.

DO WE REALLY NEED ALL THESE BRANDS OF VODKA?

No.

THE FUTURE

I predict that we will have over one hundred distilleries operating in Oregon by 2019. I believe we have already achieved world-class standards with a number of spirits (I'd nominate Clear Creek eight-year-old apple brandy, Brandy Peak aged pear brandy, McMenamins-Edgefield Pot Still brandy, Ransom's Old Tom gin and Vilya Absinthe). I believe that standards will rise for spirits produced in the state, just as they have for wine and beer, and I believe that Oregon will eventually become the standard setter for both innovation and quality in distilled spirits.

So drink Oregon spirits. Safely. In moderation. And enjoy.

Three nicely aged Oregon brandies: eight-year-old apple brandy from Clear Creek, five-year-old pear brandy from Brandy Peak and nine-year-old grape (Semillon and Pinot Noir) from McMenamins Edgefield. *Photo by the author.*

NOTES

Chapter 2

1. Scholefield and Howay, *British Columbia*, 319–20.
2. Bingham to Everts, February 16, 1829.
3. Greg Shine, Interpretation Division, U.S. Park Service, cited in Liang, "Fort Vancouver Treasures."
4. McLoughlin, *Letters of John McLoughlin*, 208.
5. Hines, *Voyage Round the World*, 21.
6. Lee and Frost, *Ten Years in Oregon*, 322.
7. Gray, *Women of the West*, 32.
8. Moss, *Pictures of Pioneer Times*, 3.
9. Those familiar with the history of Portland will recognize Pettygrove as the winner of a coin toss with Owen Lovejoy, the outcome of which would determine the name of a new town being founded on property they owned. Lovejoy wanted to name it after his hometown of Boston, Massachusetts, while Pettygrove wanted it named after his hometown of Portland, Maine.
10. Bancroft, *History of Oregon*, 1:281.
11. Clark, *Dry Years*, 15.
12. Oregon Territorial Government, *Laws of a General and Local Nature*, 95.
13. Ibid., 83.
14. Chambreau, *Biography and Recollections of Edward Chambreau.*

Chapter 3

15. Moss, *Pictures of Pioneer Times*, 55.
16. Ellendale is traditionally described as being "about two and a half miles west of Dallas." While probably true when Dallas was a lot smaller, today the location is only a half mile from the western city limits.
17. Shaw, *Story of Ellendale*, 6.
18. McClintock, "Henderson Luelling," 153–74
19. Bancroft, *History of Oregon*, 2:257.
20. Walling, *Illustrated History of Lane County*, 403.
21. Corning, *Willamette Landings*, 66, 115, 122.
22. In the United States, the depression of 1873 to 1879 was known as the Great Depression until the 1930s, when the then current crisis took the title. Those who'd been around for the first one likely weren't inclined to argue the point, being too busy trying to find food and shelter.
23. The November 23, 1906 edition of the *St. Johns Review* carried an article entitled "Portable Home Distilleries Sold in 1860 for $35" that read, "In 1860 a portable home distillery was invented that sold at a big profit for $30 to $35, and was capable of making eight to ten gallons of 'spirits' a day. The device was selling very rapidly and doing satisfactory work, when the imposition of the heavy tax on alcohol, and the restriction of its manufacture to large distilleries, whose operations could be under the eye of a government inspector, destroyed the business of the home 'stills' and they passed out of use and mind."
24. Fagan, *History of Benton County, Oregon*, 399.
25. *Eugene Guard*, "Pacific Coast News. Oregon."
26. U.S. census, 1860.
27. Dr. Mobouti was the finance minister in Nigeria during the administration of President Totali Bohgass, who was killed during a military coup in late 2015. Dr. Mobouti is in control of $35 million of treasury funds that he needs to keep out of the hands of the rebels. He would like to deposit the funds into an American bank account and offers $3.5 million to anyone providing one. All you need to do is give Dr. Mobouti access to yours, and he'll take it from there.

Chapter 4

28. "Distillery," *Oregon Sentinel.*
29. "Local Items," *Oregon Sentinel.*
30. The spent mash is referred to as "slop" in the contract. These various contracts are housed at the Southern Oregon Historical Society in Medford. They are handwritten, thankfully by someone with legible handwriting.
31. De Kergommeaux, *Canadian Whisky.*
32. Hines, *Illustrated History of the State of Oregon*, 1,148.
33. The Whiskey Trust didn't want Kidd's equipment because Medynski's still was a batch still and the trust used only column stills. The whiskey produced by the trust was similar to modern American "blended whiskey," being nearly all neutral spirit mixed with a small amount of bourbon, plus some burnt sugar to darken the color. "Blended whiskey" from Canada, Ireland and Scotland is made using grain whiskey, which is distilled at a proof lower than neutral spirit and aged in barrels; only in the United States can you bottle something that is 80 percent vodka and call it whiskey. Is this a great country or what?
34. Hines, *Illustrated History of the State of Oregon*, 1,148.
35. "Big Enterprise," *Jacksonville Democratic Times.*
36. "Brevities," *Ashland Tidings.*
37. "Local News" *Medford Mail.*
38. The distributor in San Francisco was the Lilienthal family, whose daughter married into the Haas family, bringing the California distribution rights with her. The Haas family has recently reintroduced Cyrus Noble, sourcing from an unnamed Kentucky distillery.
39. "Medford Bartender Is Acquitted," *Morning Oregonian.*

Chapter 5

40. *Adjutant & Inspector General of the State of Vermont*, 1,070.
41. Vermont, Vital Records, 3,748.
42. IRS annual report, 1892, 148.
43. "Distillery Burns," *Capital Journal.*
44. Ibid.
45. "Village Destroyed," *Los Angeles Herald.*
46. "Goldendale Wants the Distillery," *Dalles Daily Chronicle.*

Chapter 6

47. Caswell, "Prohibition Movement in Oregon, Part 1," 245.
48. Ibid., 251.
49. Ibid., 252.
50. John, "War on the Webfoot Saloon."
51. Ibid.
52. Ibid.
53. Caswell, "Prohibition Movement in Oregon, Part 1," 261.
54. Ibid., "Prohibition Movement in Oregon, Part 2," 66.
55. Ibid., 67.
56. "Jurors Said to Have Drunk Whiskey Exhibits," *La Grande Evening Observer*.
57. Mattoon, *Baptist Annals of Oregon*, 392.
58. "Oregon Moonshiners," *Morning Oregonian*.
59. Oregon Blue Book, "Initiative, Referendum and Recall: 1912–1914."
60. Swenson, "Intrepid Miss Hobbs," 15.
61. Fern Hobbs was formidable in will, not stature, standing five feet, four inches tall, and weighing less than one hundred pounds.
62. Swenson, "Intrepid Miss Hobbs," 15.
63. Caswell, "Prohibition Movement in Oregon, Part 2," 78.
64. Oregon Blue Book, "Initiative, Referendum and Recall: 1912–1914."

Chapter 7

65. "Limit on Liquor Is Held Illegal," *Morning Oregonian*.
66. Oregon Blue Book, "Initiative, Referendum and Recall: 1916–1921."
67. Churchill, "Mr. Churchill's Compilation of Alcohol Sales by Druggists."
68. Chandler and Kennedy, *Murder and Scandal in Prohibition Portland*, 15, 72.
69. Marsh, *20 Years a Soldier of Fortune*, 187.
70. Ibid., 181.
71. Asbury, *Great Illusion*, 135.
72. "Third Circus Bandit Probably Identified," *Morning Oregonian*.
73. Hanks, Bureau of Prohibition Memorandum to the Bureau Field Division.
74. Ibid.
75. Ibid., Report to U.S. Attorney George Neuner, Case 131-M, 3–10.
76. Ibid., 11–28.
77. Ibid., 29–43.

78. Ibid., 44–51.
79. Cohoon, Report to Special Agent in Charge R. A. Beman.
80. "Honor Among Bootleggers Not Reliable," *Morning Oregonian*.
81. Chandler and Kennedy, *Murder and Scandal in Prohibition Portland*, 117.
82. "Fat Profit Made in Liquor Racket," *Morning Oregonian*.
83. Murphy, Report to the Director of the Bureau of Prohibition, 2.
84. Braly, *Tales from the Oregon Outback*, 34.
85. Nelson, *Memoirs of an Oregon Moonshiner*, 26.
86. Chandler and Kennedy, *Murder and Scandal in Prohibition Portland*, 125.
87. Oregon Blue Book, "Initiative, Referendum and Recall: 1930–1936."

Chapter 8

88. Oregon Liquor Control Commission, *Oregon Liquor Control Act (The Knox Law) and Liquor Revenue Act*.
89. Internal Revenue Service, Bureau of Internal Revenue report, July 19, 1934.
90. Asheville School Yearbook, 1907–1908.
91. Dameron, "Albert William Peters—Facts."
92. Linné Dodge of Hood River Distillers, interview with the author, October 28, 2014.
93. Linné Dodge, personal communication to author, June 3, 2016.
94. Hall, *Wines of the Pacific Northwest*, 64.
95. "Washington, Oregon, Buy Up Distilleries," *Southeast Missourian*.

Chapter 9

96. Steve McCarthy, interview with the author, May 21, 2016. Unless otherwise noted, all information in this chapter is from this interview.
97. The BATF was transferred to the Department of Justice in 2003, after which the IRS's Alcohol and Tobacco Tax and Trade Bureau (TTB) took over the licensing, regulation and taxation of distilleries.
98. Rachel Inman of Clear Creek, interview with the author, May 21, 2016.

Chapter 10

99. Seth Yorra, personal communication with the author, July 25, 2016.
100. David and Georgia Nowlin, interview with the author, June 9, 2016.
101. Jim Bendis, personal communication with the author, June 22, 2016.
102. Tad Seestedt, interview with the author, June 28, 2016.
103. Clark McCool, interview with the author, June 27, 2016.
104. RMS was another California brandy producer, being a joint venture by the cognac house Remy-Martin and Napa Valley sparkling wine producer Schramsberg. The venture ended in 2002, probably because Remy-Martin believed RMS sales were cutting into those of its cognac.
105. Christian Krogstad, interview with the author, July 12, 2016.
106. Tom Burkleaux, personal communication with the author, August 16, 2016.
107. "Cottage Grove Distillery Finds Winning Mix of Vodka, Charity," *Medford Mail Tribune.*
108. "Owner of Distillery Faces Sentencing for Tax Evasion," *Eugene Register-Guard.*
109. John Ufford, telephone interview with the author, July 2016.
110. Jacques Tardy, interview with the author, July 2016.
111. Michelle Ly, interview with the author, July 12, 2016.
112. Dan Stein, interview with the author, October 29, 2014.

Chapter 11

113. Most of the information in this chapter comes from interviews conducted with Dudley Clark and with his former partner, along with notes taken by the author over the years.

Chapter 12

114. Distillery counts from IRS TTB; population counts from U.S. census.
115. Statista.com, "Craft Beer Breweries Per Capita in the United States in 2015, by State."
116. Information compiled via industry database searches at winesandvines.com.
117. Infante and Kolmar, "What's America's Booziest State?"

118. Rentfrow, Gosling, Jokela, Stillwell, Kosinski and Potter, "Divided We Stand."
119. 16personalities, "Personality Geography of the United States."
120. Lipka and Wormald, "How Religious Is Your State?"
121. Fottrell, "This Is the Atheist Capital of America."
122. Foyston, "New Guild Raises Its Glass to Oregon Distillers."
123. Christie Scott, OLCC Alcohol Program Spokesperson, interview with the author, August 9, 2016.

BIBLIOGRAPHY

The Adjutant & Inspector General of the State of Vermont, Report of, 1863–1866. Ancestry.com.

Asbury, Herbert. *The Great Illusion: An Informal History of Prohibition.* New York: Doubleday & Co., 1950.

Asheville School Yearbook, 1907–1908. The Asheville School, Asheville, NC.

Ashland Tidings. "Brevities." November 20, 1891, 3.

Bancroft, Hubert Howe. *History of Oregon.* Vols. 1–2. San Francisco, CA: History Company, 1888.

Bingham, H., to J. Everts, February 16, 1829. In *Oregon Historical Quarterly* 30 (September 1929): 264–65.

Braly, David. *Tales from the Oregon Outback.* Prineville, OR: American Media Co., 1978.

Capital Journal. "Distillery Burns." April 8, 1892.

Caswell, John E. "The Prohibition Movement in Oregon, Part 1." *Oregon Historical Quarterly* 39, no. 3 (1938): 235–61.

———. "The Prohibition Movement in Oregon, Part 2." *Oregon Historical Quarterly* 40, no. 1 (1939): 64–82.

Chambreau, Williams Wadhams. *Biography and Recollections of Edward Chambreau.* 1937. http://chambreauresources.com/ned/life.htm.

Chandler, J.D., and Theresa Griffin Kennedy. *Murder and Scandal in Prohibition Portland.* Charleston, SC: The History Press, 2016.

BIBLIOGRAPHY

Churchill, Percy. "Mr. Churchill's Compilation of Alcohol Sales by Druggists (Information taken from books at County Clerk's Office)." October 23, 1916, City of Portland Municipal Archives, Portland, OR.

Clark, Norman H. *The Dry Years*. Seattle: University of Washington Press, 1965.

Cohoon, B.W. Report to Special Agent in Charge R. A. Beman, June 27, 1930. Records of the Department of the Treasury. Record Group 56. Bureau of Prohibition. Investigatory Case Files 1924–33. National Archives at Seattle, WA.

Corning, Howard McKinley. *Willamette Landings*. 2nd ed. Portland: Oregon Historical Society, 1973.

Crain, Liz. *Food Lover's Guide to Portland*. Seattle, WA: Sasquatch Books, 2010.

The Dalles Daily Chronicle. "Goldendale Wants the Distillery." July 17, 1894, 1.

Dameron, Elizabeth. "Albert William Peters—Facts." http://person. ancestry.com/tree/289535/person/-2099491888/facts.

De Kergommeaux, Davin. *Canadian Whisky*. http://www.canadianwhisky.org.

Eugene Guard. "Pacific Coast News. Oregon." December 10, 1870.

Eugene Register-Guard, "Owner of Distillery Faces Sentencing for Tax Evasion." November 3, 2012.

Fagan, David. *History of Benton County, Oregon*. Portland, OR: A.G. Walling, 1885.

Fottrell, Quentin. "This Is the Atheist Capital of America." http://www.marketwatch.com/story/this-is-the-most-godless-city-in-america-2015-03-24.

Foyston, John. "New Guild Raises Its Glass to Oregon Distillers." *Oregonlive/The Oregonian*, June 7, 2008, http://www.oregonlive.com/business/oregonian/index.ssf?/base/business/1212803743214750.xml&coll=7.

Gray, Dorothy. *Women of the West*. Lincoln: University of Nebraska Press, 1976.

Hall, Lisa Shara. *Wines of the Pacific Northwest*. London: Mitchell Beazley, 2001.

Hanks, Melvin L. Bureau of Prohibition Memorandum to the Bureau Field Division, March 1, 1928. Records of the Department of the Treasury. Record Group 56. Bureau of Prohibition. Investigatory Case Files 1924–33. The National Archives at Seattle, WA.

Hanks, Melvin L. Report to U.S. Attorney George Neuner, Case 131-M, August 27, 1928. Records of the Department of the Treasury. Record Group 56. Bureau of Prohibition. Investigatory Case Files 1924–33. The National Archives at Seattle, WA.

Hines, Gustavus. *A Voyage Round the World: With a History of the Oregon Mission*. Buffalo, NY: George Derby and Company, 1850.

BIBLIOGRAPHY

Hines, H.K. *An Illustrated History of the State of Oregon*. Chicago: Lewis Publishing Company, 1893.

Infante, Dave, and Chris Kolmar. "What's America's Booziest State?" *Thrillist*, November 16, 2014. https://www.thrillist.com/drink/nation/which-us-state-drinks-the-most-booziest-states.

Internal Revenue Service. *Annual Report of the Commissioner of Internal Revenue*. Reports from 1863 through 1917.

———. Bureau of Internal Revenue Report, July 19, 1934. Records of the Department of the Treasury. Record Group 56. Bureau of Prohibition. Investigatory Case Files 1924–33. The National Archives at Seattle.

Jacksonville Democratic Times. "A Big Enterprise." May 22, 1891, 3.

John, Finn J.D. "The War on the Webfoot Saloon." http://wicked-portland.com/lost-chapter.html.

La Grande Evening Observer. "Jurors Said to Have Drunk Whiskey Exhibits." September 14, 1910, 1.

Lee, D. and J.H. Frost. *Ten Years in Oregon*. New York: self-published, 1844.

Liang, Michael. "Fort Vancouver Treasures." *Ranger Mike Designs: Inspiration for the National Park Service*, January 21, 2010. rangermikedesigns.wordpress.com/2010/01/21/fort-vancouver-treasures.

Lipka, Michael, and Benjamin Wormald. "How Religious Is Your State?" PEW Research Center. February 29, 2016. http://www.pewresearch.org/fact-tank/2016/02/29/how-religious-is-your-state.

Los Angeles Herald. "A Village Destroyed." June 14, 1894, 1.

Marsh, Floyd R. *20 Years a Soldier of Fortune*. Portland, OR: Thomas Binford, 1976.

Mattoon, Charles Hiram. *Baptist Annals of Oregon*. Vol. 2. McMinnville, OR: Telephone Register Publishing Company, 1913.

McClintock, Thomas C. "Henderson Luelling, Seth Lewelling and the Birth of the Pacific Coast Fruit Industry." *Oregon Historical Quarterly* 60, no. 2 (1967): 153–74.

McLoughlin, John. *The Letters of John McLoughlin from Fort Vancouver to the Governor and Committee : First Series, 1825–38*. Toronto, ON: Champlain Society for the Hudson's Bay Record Society, 1941.

Medford Mail. "Local News." January 14, 1892, 3.

Medford Mail Tribune. "Cottage Grove Distillery Finds Winning Mix of Vodka, Charity." May 12, 2008.

Morning Oregonian. "Fat Profit Made in Liquor Racket." December 6, 1928.

———. "Honor Among Bootleggers Not Reliable." December 5, 1928.

———. "Limit on Liquor Is Held Illegal." July 26, 1916, 1.

———. "Medford Bartender Is Acquitted." January 25, 1903, 6.

BIBLIOGRAPHY

———. "Oregon Moonshiners." October 8, 1911.

———. "Third Circus Bandit Probably Identified." September 20, 1921, 5.

Moss, Sidney. *Pictures of Pioneer Times at Oregon City*. Oregon City, OR: self-published, 1878.

Murphy, Charles A. Report to the Director of the Bureau of Prohibition, September 24, 1930, 2. Records of the Department of the Treasury. Record Group 56. Bureau of Prohibition. Investigatory Case Files 1924–33. The National Archives at Seattle, WA.

Nelson, Ray. *Memoirs of an Oregon Moonshiner*. N.p.: self-published, 1976.

Oregon Blue Book. "Initiative, Referendum and Recall: 1916–1921." http://bluebook.state.or.us/state/elections/elections13.htm.

———. "Initiative, Referendum and Recall: 1930–1936." http://bluebook.state.or.us/state/elections/elections15.htm.

———. "Initiative, Referendum and Recall: 1912–1914." http://bluebook.state.or.us/state/elections/elections12.htm.

Oregon Liquor Control Commission. *Oregon Liquor Control Act (The Knox Law) and Liquor Revenue Act*. 1935. Compiled by the OLCC.

Oregon Sentinel. "Distillery." August 19, 1882.

———. "Local Items." March 18, 1883.

Oregon Territorial Government. *Laws of a General and Local Nature Passed by the Legislative Committee and Legislative Assembly 1843–1849*. 1853. Oregon State Archives, Salem, OR.

Rentfrow, Peter J., Samuel D. Gosling, Markus Jokela, David J. Stillwell, Michal Kosinski and Jeff Potter. "Divided We Stand: Three Psychological Regions of the United States and Their Political, Economic, Social, and Health Correlates." *Journal of Personality and Social Psychology* 105, no. 6 (2013): 996–1,012.

Scholefield, E.O.S., and F.W. Howay. *British Columbia: From the Earliest Times to the Present*. Vol. 1. Vancouver, BC: S.J. Clarke, 1914.

Shaw, Claud L. *The Story of Ellendale*. 1911. Reprinted in the journal of the Polk County Historical Society *Historically Speaking* 10 (1992): 6–7.

16personalities. "Personality Geography of the United States." https://www.16personalities.com/articles/personality-geography-of-the-united-states.

Southeast Missourian. "Washington, Oregon, Buy Up Distilleries." December 1, 1943.

Statista.com. "Craft Beer Breweries Per Capita in the United States in 2015, by State." http://www.statista.com/statistics/319978/craft-beer-breweries-per-capita-in-the-us-by-state.

BIBLIOGRAPHY

Stewart, Amy. *The Drunken Botanist.* Chapel Hill, NC: Algonquin Books, 2013.

Swenson, Eric D. "The Intrepid Miss Hobbs." *Willamette Lawyer* 7, no. 1 (2007): 15.

U.S. Census, 1860. Ancestry.com.

Vermont. Vital Records, 1720–1908. ancestry.com.

Walling, Albert. *An Illustrated History of Lane County.* Portland, OR: A.G. Walling, 1884.

Winesandvines.com. Industry database search engine.

INDEX

INDEX

INDEX

INDEX

ABOUT THE AUTHOR

Scott Stursa's longtime passion for fine food and drink combined with a keen interest in spirits production make him uniquely qualified to assess Oregon's distilleries and their products. He has written about these topics on his blog (www. oregonepicurean.com) and has researched the history of the state's liquor industry, activities that until recently were secondary to a demanding career in cyber security. Now unencumbered by that vocation, he has been able to focus his attention on research and writing, and *Distilled in Oregon* is the result. Scott lives in Corvallis, Oregon, with his wife and their two cats and is currently working on a novel.

Visit us at
www.historypress.net
....
This title is also available as an e-book